Best iPhone Apps
The Guide for Discriminating Downloaders

by Josh Clark

O'REILLY®

Beijing · Cambridge · Farnham · Köln · Sebastopol · Taipei · Tokyo

Best iPhone Apps: The Guide for Discriminating Downloaders
by Josh Clark

Copyright © 2009 Josh Clark
Printed in Canada.

Published by O'Reilly Media, Inc., 1005 Gravenstein Highway North, Sebastopol, CA 95472.

O'Reilly books may be purchased for educational, business, or sales promotional use. Online editions are also available for most titles (http://my.safaribooksonline.com). For more information, contact our corporate/institutional sales department: (800) 998-9938 or corporate@oreilly.com.

Editor: Peter Meyers

Production Editor: Nellie McKesson

Design: Josh Clark, Edie Freedman, and Nellie McKesson

Printing History:
First Edition: July 2009

ISBN: 978-0-596-80427-5

[TM]

[10/09]

Contents

Contents

Contents

Foreword

My elementary school in Minneapolis had sensational student assemblies. It wasn't the stock parade of Just Say No and Scared Straight folks, or the usual collection of career-day speakers. We got a swami. We got a Secret Service agent. I'm just saying: We had great assemblies. One of them, though, stuck with me more than the rest.

It was 1977. I don't remember the speaker's name, but he made music—electronic music, with big, heavy equipment. His gear filled the stage of our homely auditorium, and he sprang from machine to machine to make this weird music of blips and bleeps and eerie organ sounds. He knew how to warm up an under-10 crowd; Star Wars had arrived in theaters that spring, and he used his outrageously fancy equipment to boom R2-D2 sounds at us, all chirps and whistles. He owned us.

At the end, he stepped to the front of the stage. "One day," he said, "all of you will be able to have a machine that does all this, makes music like this." He pulled out his wallet and held it up. "And it will fit in your pocket." I'll never forget it: "It will fit in your pocket." I was six years old, and it was the first time I really ached for a specific vision of the future. For me, the future wasn't rocket cars. It wasn't living on the moon. It wasn't even R2-D2. The future was having my own little synthesizer, a computer in my pocket to make stuff.

And so I waited, for three decades, until the iPhone finally arrived in 2007. Apple's fabulous device is the only thing that's ever resembled my childhood notions of the 21st century, the first time the future finally got here. A computer. In your pocket. That helps you makes stuff. People are using iPhones to paint, to compose music, to write novels… and sure, to goof off, too, to connect with friends and interact with their surroundings in entirely new ways. Add to that all the magical things that we've already begun to take for granted: plucking information and video from thin air; taking commands by voice or touch; mapping out the world around us. Now we're talking. This is what my mystery man from 1977 was getting at.

But the future came on so fast that it's a little overwhelming. After two years of living and working with my prized iPhone, I'm still discovering and marveling at the things it can do. Nearly every iPhone owner I know is paralyzed by the options in the App Store, more than 70,000 apps at last count. We're awash in the future.

I wrote this book to help you stay ahead of the current. I scoured the App Store to find the best apps that will make your iPhone shine and make you more productive, more creative, more happy. Try as many of them as you can, play a little, discover what your magical device can do. This is the future we're talking about, after all. It's here, and it fits in your pocket.

Happy downloading.

About the Author

Josh Clark is a writer, designer, and developer who helps creative people get clear of technical hassles to share their ideas with the world. When he's not writing about clever design and humane software, he's building it. Josh is the creator of Big Medium, friendly software that actually makes it fun to manage websites. In a previous life, Josh worked on a slew of national PBS programs at Boston's WGBH. He shared his three words of Russian with Mikhail Gorbachev, strolled the ranch with Nancy Reagan, and wrote trivia questions for a primetime game show. Now Josh makes words and spins code at his hypertext laboratory *www.globalmoxie.com*. He welcomes your feedback at *jclark@globalmoxie.com*.

Best Apps at Work

 Your iPhone's elegant design may drip with sophistication, but don't let its pretty face fool you: This is one gadget that's not afraid to muscle in and get its hands dirty with serious work. Whether you're wrangling projects, hoisting spreadsheets, slinging documents, or crunching numbers, your workhorse iPhone has the brawn and know-how to help make quick work of the job at hand.

This chapter shows you how to turn your iPhone or iPod Touch into a paragon of productivity. Download the best apps for **getting stuff done** to help manage your time, to-do lists, ideas, and work environment. Show off your remarkable talent for **juggling documents** with apps that let you create, share, and sync files from the palm of your hand. And in all this app-addled excitement, don't forget that your capable little iPhone is actually, y'know, a phone, too… You'll learn about apps for **making calls** easier, cheaper, and faster. You'll finish up with a crash course in **advanced geekery,** where you'll discover such arcane secrets as how to use your iPhone or iPod Touch to access your computer from miles or even continents away.

So stop lollygagging, and get to business. A new day of productivity lies ahead.

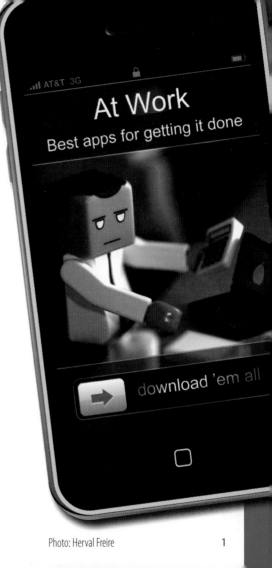

Photo: Herval Freire

1

Best App for To-Do Lists

Things

$9.99
Version: 1.3.10
Cultured Code

The App Store is chockablock with to-do lists, but Things sets itself apart in flexibility and ease. Organization systems are hugely personal, and Things adapts easily to your own approach, growing with you as your needs (and to-do list) expand. Keep it simple with a single checklist, or juggle a sprawling collection of projects, responsibilities, and contexts, staged over time. As complex as your tasks might be, Things makes it easy to manage them.

LIST OF LISTS: Organize to-dos into lists or projects. New items land in Inbox until you put them in a list. Tap Today to see your front-burner tasks (due items also appear there automatically). The Next list shows the full rundown of all your active to-dos. Stage tasks in the Scheduled list to start on a specific date, or use the Someday list to park items for the vague and hazy future. Tap Projects to review tasks by individual project.

COLLECT 'EM ALL: Things makes it easy to collect new to-dos to get them out of your head fast. Call up the New To Do screen by tapping the + button at the bottom left of any other screen. Type the name of the task and you're done; or add additional details as shown here. Tag it with a category (for contexts like errand, home, work, priority, and so on), add notes, set a due date, or assign the task to a specific project or list.

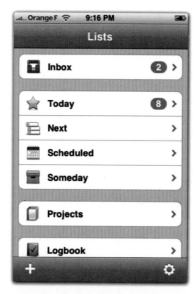

At Work

2

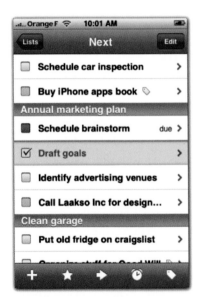

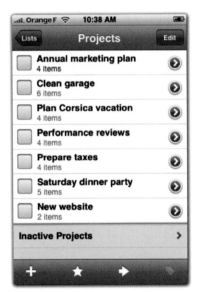

UP NEXT: Select a list to review its tasks. Here, the Next list shows your entire list of active to-dos (don't panic!). Yellow shows tasks in your Today list; red items are due. Tap a task's checkbox to mark it done, or tap its name to edit the task. In the bottom icon menu, tap the star to mark tasks for today, the arrow to move them to a new list, the clock to sort by due date, or the tag to filter by category (for tasks tagged "work," for example).

PROJECT PRO: Use Projects to manage more complex goals, collecting their to-dos into individual lists. In the Projects screen shown here, tap a project to see all of its tasks. Projects with due items are highlighted in red. Mark a project complete—along with any of its remaining tasks—by tapping its checkbox. Tap Inactive Projects to see the list of projects you've stashed in your Scheduled or Someday list.

The Task at Hand

A to-do list is useful only when you actually have it with you, which is why your iPhone is an ideal place to keep your tasks within reach. More than a notebook, a desktop computer, or a messy collection of Post-it notes, your phone probably never leaves your side (especially not your prized iPhone). With an app like Things, that means it's always convenient to refer to your list or add a new task—no matter where you are.

Even so, you might want your lists in a different format—in print or on your computer. For that, Mac users can sync Things with the software's equally excellent desktop version (available from *culturedcode.com*). If you don't use a Mac and syncing is a priority, take a peek at the runner-up apps on the next page.

Other Apps for To-Do Lists

Todo

$9.99 (free demo available)
Version: 3.0
Appigo

Remember the Milk

Free, but requires $25/year subscription
Version: 1.1.1
Remember the Milk

Todo does everything you'd want in a to-do list—and almost certainly more. With so many features, fields, colors, icons, and customization options, Todo lacks the easy elegance that earns Things the top pick in this category. But Todo has a nifty set of bells and whistles that hardcore organizers may consider essential.

Todo is great at talking to other online and desktop to-do lists. Sync your web-based lists at *toodledo.com* or *rememberthemilk.com*, or use Appigo's free software to sync with iCal for Mac; similar software is planned for Outlook. Other features you won't find in Things: Subcategorize to-do lists; label tasks with tags, priorities, *or* contexts (in Things, you use tags for all three); add repeating tasks like monthly rent or weekly trash pickup; get alerts when tasks are due; and customize list colors, completed task graphics, and priority icons. Especially cool: "task types" let you turn to-dos into one-tap actions to call, email, text, or map a contact.

Rememberthemilk.com is cool and refreshing, a justly popular website for managing to-do lists. Like Todo, the site's official app lets you work with your online task list, provided you've purchased the site's $25/year "pro" account (you get a 15-day free trial). As you might expect, the official app is more tailored to the site's features than Todo and makes the best fit for devoted RTM fans.

The app adds a location feature not offered in Things or Todo, letting you link tasks to nearby places where you can tackle 'em: When you're near the grocery store, Remember the Milk reminds you to, yes, remember the milk. The standard setup emphasizes due dates more than the other apps, with dock icons to quickly view tasks due today, tomorrow, or this week. You can customize the dock icons for other views, including lists, tags, nearby location, and a search feature that lets you save common searches.

Best App for Tracking Big Goals

Goal Tender

$2.99
Version: 1.0.5
Roobasoft

Don't let the small things you've gotta do today make you forget your grand plans for tomorrow. Goal Tender is a little app about the big picture, a tidy complement to the nitty-gritty task managers of the last few pages. Tap in the goal to accomplish, and watch the progress bar surge as you wind your way to completion. The app optionally stores your goals online, too, letting you see them in your Outlook 2007, iCal, or Google calendar.

GOAL IN SIGHT: Goal Tender's main screen lists your goals, along with due-date countdowns and your progress to completion. Add daily or weekly tasks to each of these big goals to help stay on track with bite-sized actions. Here, the "Read Crime & Punishment" goal has a daily "Read a chapter" task. Tap the Someday tab to browse long-term dreams, so you don't lose track of that goal to dogsled the Yukon.

PILGRIM'S PROGRESS: As you make your journey to your goal's completion, slide the progress bar in the goal's Details screen to show how far you've come. Every goal has its own journal where you can record your efforts and discoveries. This screen is also where you can add related weekly or daily goals.

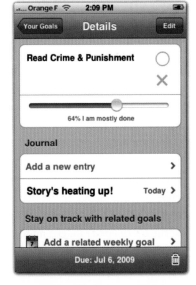

Best App for Remembering Stuff

reQall
Free
Version: 2.0.4
QTech

Turn your iPhone into an unfailing executive assistant, ready to remind you of calendar items, notes, and to-dos. It's almost magic: Say, "Meet Rich at 4:30 pm tomorrow," and reQall transcribes the text, creates a to-do, adds an event to your calendar, and sends you a reminder before the meeting. It's like an outboard memory for the overloaded modern mind. The app requires a free account at *reqall.com*.

SPEAK YOUR MIND: Don't just mutter about all the things you've got to do, say it out loud to reQall. Tap the Add screen, speak for up to 30 seconds, and the app transcribes your words over the Internet. Within a couple of minutes, the text appears on your to-do list, filed in all the appropriate places. You can also type reminders or submit them via instant message, toll-free call, or email (email requires a paid reQall "pro" account).

TIME-CONSCIOUS: ReQall scours your messages for meaning. Mention a time, date, or day, and the app queues a reminder. The *reqall.com* website lets you choose how to receive these alerts. Ask to receive reminders via email or instant message; pro accounts ($3/month or $25/year) can receive SMS texts, too. The website also lets you set up your Outlook, iCal, or Google calendar to see your reminders there as well.

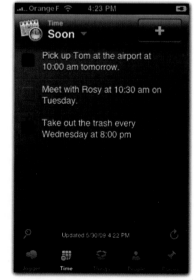

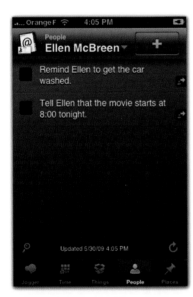

SHARE THE LOVE: Send reminders to friends, family, and coworkers, too—anyone from your iPhone's contact list. Once added to reQall, the app recognizes their names and sends them reminders when you start a message with "remind," "tell," or "ask." Your freshly reminded pals receive these alerts by email; they'll also see a notice in their account lists if they happen to use reQall, too.

DULY NOTED: Start your message with the word "note," and reQall stashes the message away as note text for future reference. ReQall's transcription is impressively accurate, but even when it's off, you can always edit the text or listen to the original recording. Tap any note or reminder to bring up the Details screen to edit or listen, or to add due date, location, or a contact with whom you want to share.

A FAST JOG: The Memory Jogger screen filters your reminders to show the items most relevant to the current place and time. Paid pro accounts can set up locations so that when you say "at work," for example, the reminder pops up in Memory Jogger when you're at your desk.

Best App for Tracking Time

Jobs
$1.99
Version: 1.2
Bjango

Time is money, especially if you're a freelance designer or an hour-tallying lawyer. When you need exact counts of billable hours—or just want to track how you spend your time— Jobs watches the clock for you. Add all your projects to the app, and run the stopwatch for a job while you're working on it. When you're ready to send a bill, email yourself the timesheet info in one of several formats to whip up your invoice.

ON THE CLOCK: The Jobs screen shows all your current projects. Tap the stopwatch next to a job's name to start a time session for the job, and tap again to stop. The red badge in the dock icon shows how many stopwatches are running. The app's icon also shows this tally on the home screen of your iPhone or iPod Touch; the app keeps the clock running even when it's not active. Cool.

TIME TALLY: Tap a job to see the Job Details screen, which shows the total time and earnings for the job so far. Tap the blue Play button to start the timer, and tap again to stop. This screen also lets you set the big-picture info for the job, including notes, client, and your hourly rate. The Flagfall field lets you set a starting fee for the job, and the app counts up from there. To email yourself timesheet data, tap Export Job.

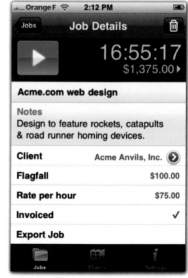

At Work

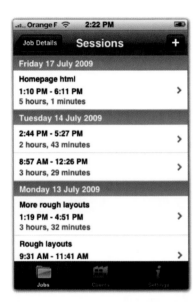

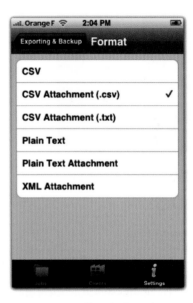

JAM SESSIONS: The Sessions screen lets you review and edit a job's individual time sessions. Tap a session to add a descriptive name for that period or to edit the start or stop time. If you forgot to run your timer for part of the job, get your time back by tapping the + button at top right to add a session manually. Alas, you can view sessions only for one job; there's no way to see today's sessions across all jobs, for example.

CUSTOMER FOCUS: Choose a client from the app's Clients screen to see all the jobs for that client (tapping a job takes you to its detail screen). You can link a client to an entry from the Contacts app, giving you one-tap access to your customer's contact info. Tap Export to pluck out the timesheet info for the jobs shown.

EXPERT EXPORT: All your hard-earned time data doesn't do much good if you leave it trapped in your phone. Jobs lets you email the data in several formats, including CSV (for editing in a spreadsheet), plain text, or XML. The app lets you choose whether to include individual session info or just the bottom-line tally. When the data arrives in your inbox, pour it into your invoice and start cashing in on those long hours.

Best App for Tracking Packages

Delivery Status Touch
$2.99
Version: 2.3.3
Junecloud

Who knew tracking deliveries could be so classy? This stylish, efficient app tracks packages from over 40 stores and delivery services, even mapping your package's current-ish location. Set up a free account at the app's website to sync tracking info; once done, you can paste or bookmark tracking numbers from your computer instead of tapping them into your iPhone.

SPECIAL DELIVERY: The app's screen counts down the delivery of all your packages, color-coded by store or parcel service. Tap the number or icon for a package to see complete order details from the shipper, including a View Map button to see the package inching your way. Add or delete packages from the list by tapping the Info icon at bottom right.

MISTER POSTMAN: Delivery Status Touch supports a long list of services. You can track orders mailed from stores like Amazon, Apple, or Nintendo, for example, or track directly with the carrier for a wide range of US and international parcel services, including the US Postal Service, UPS, FedEx, DHL, TNT, and even the Italian postal service.

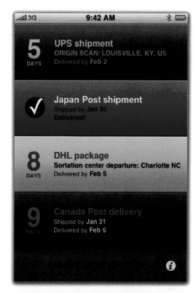

Best App for Working the Web

Google Mobile App
Free
Version: 0.3.1448
Google

So you might've heard. There's this company called Google that knows a thing or two about Web search, and they've figured it out for iPhone, too, with the best app for searching the Web. The secret ingredient is voice search. Just talk into your iPhone or microphone-enabled iPod Touch, and the app fetches the results for your spoken keywords. Tap a result to launch Mobile Safari and you're in business.

TALKING POINTS: Searching the Web has never been so easy. Just lift the phone to your ear, wait for the tone, and say what you're looking for. Google's a good listener, and the speech recognition is excellent. But there are rewards to tapping out your search phrase instead: The app suggests a list of popular searches or additional keywords to hone your search. Google also suggests matches from your contact list or past searches.

LOCAL COLOR: Your iPhone always knows where you are, and Google Mobile App puts that info to work to show you results for your surroundings. Search for "weather" to see the local forecast for your location, for example, or "movie showtimes" to find out what's playing in the area. Likewise, if you start tapping out a search for "restaurants," Google offers to find places nearby to grab a bite.

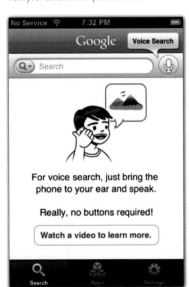

Best App for Brainstorming

iThoughts
$7.99
Version: 1.10
CMS

Cross an outline with a flow chart, and you get a "mind map," a visual sketch for capturing and organizing stream-of-consciousness ideas. iThoughts diagrams these brainstorm sessions on your iPhone. A bubble represents your topic; draw links to more bubbles for related ideas, which grow like tendrils across the screen. When you're done, prune and organize branches into shape. Email or share maps online in several formats.

BRANCH OUT: Start with a central idea—starting a new career as a superhero, for example—and add branches for the concepts and topics to consider. The diagram sprouts clouds and tentacles of topics and subtopics. iThoughts provides a big canvas for your mind map, about 100 iPhone screens. Swipe to move around, pinch to make the map larger or smaller, or flip your iPhone or iPod on its side for landscape view.

BUBBLING WITH IDEAS: Tap a bubble to select it (here, "Billionaire playboy" is selected). Toolbars materialize to let you add a subtopic bubble or add another bubble at the same level. Tap the arrow at top right (or double-tap the bubble) to edit an item's text, color, shape, or add an icon. You can drag bubbles anywhere on the map, or cut, copy, and paste them into different branches, along with any subtopic bubbles.

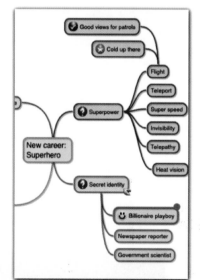

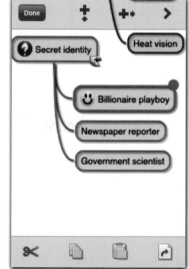

At Work

TAKE NOTE: Bubble text is typically brief, but iThoughts lets you attach longer notes to any item, including a link to a web page, phone number, or email address. Select a bubble with a note, and its text appears at the bottom of the screen, as shown here for the "secret identity" bubble. When the selected bubble has subtopics, tap the blue arrow icon to show or hide those subtopic bubbles.

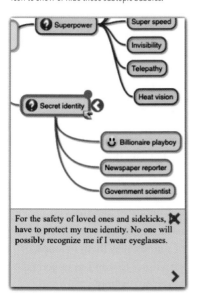

Outliner

$2.99
Version: 1.5.2
CarbonFin

If the freeform sprawl of mind maps makes you antsy, fall back to more traditional methods. Outliner lets you create and share outlines in an effortless interface that lets you get your ideas down fast. Change an item to a task, and Outliner adds a checkbox so you can mark it done after you've knocked it off your list. Email your outline as plain text or OPML, a format for sharing with desktop outline software. You can also sync and share outlines online with a free account at the app's website, where you invite others to come admire your clear, organized ideas.

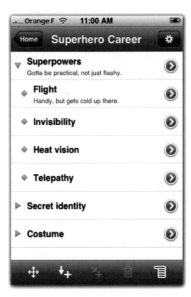

OUTSTANDING OUTLINES: Create an outline of topics and subtopics. Tap one of the + icons in the dock to add an item at the same level as the selected topic, or to create a subtopic. Move a topic in the outline by tapping the four-point compass arrow; you can indent, outdent, or move it higher or lower in the list. Tap the blue arrow for an item to edit it, add a note, or turn the item into a task for your to-do list.

Best App for Shutting Out Noise

SoundCurtain

$3.99
Version: 1.2
FutureAcoustic

Got a cubicle neighbor yammering on the phone? Jackhammers going strong outside? SoundCurtain quiets the din so that you can focus on work (or catch some shuteye). The app uses your iPhone's microphone to analyze the surrounding sound and play a corresponding level of ambient music or white noise, covering distracting sounds with something more soothingly relaxing.

NOISE BUSTER: Plug a microphone into your iPhone or iPod Touch (the standard iPhone headphones work just fine), and SoundCurtain plays one of five audio themes, adjusting the levels to compensate for surrounding noise. The "Rain Masker" theme is especially soothing, but you can choose from other sounds, including two that play new-agey harmonic tunes. Tap the screen to call up settings to adjust sound level and sensitivity.

 HONORABLE MENTION

Ambiance

$4.99
Version: 2.1
Matt Coneybeare

Unlike SoundCurtain, Ambiance doesn't respond to the surrounding environment. Instead it simply provides a big, big collection of calming sounds to drown out the clamor around you. Think iTunes for zen audio. The app comes loaded with three sounds—rain, wind chimes, and loon calls—and you can download more from a free library of hundreds of tension-melting clips. Make a mix of sounds, play them in loops, or set a timer to stop—after you fall asleep, for example.

Best App for Offbeat Inspiration

Oblique Strategies

Free
Version: 1.0.1
Far Out Labs

When writer's block strikes or procrastination descends, this app helps you tackle your project from a fresh direction. In 1975, musician Brian Eno and artist Peter Schmidt published a deck of cards titled "Oblique Strategies: One Hundred Worthwhile Dilemmas." Each card featured an enigmatic phrase to help break creative deadlocks by suggesting a fresh mindset. This app reproduces all five editions of the card set, letting you draw a fresh idea from the top of the stack when inspiration runs dry.

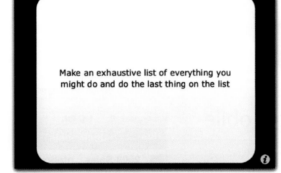

Make an exhaustive list of everything you might do and do the last thing on the list

Gardening, not architecture

PRACTICAL STEPS: Some cards suggest a practical exercise to jog your mind and nudge you out of your rut. "Take a break," one card advises. "Go outside. Shut the door," counsels another. Hey, if you're stuck, you're stuck. What've you got to lose?

OBSCURE HINTS: Most of the cards contain cryptic phrases to remind you that there's more than one way to approach a problem. Here, the card seems to suggest that a more organic approach might be better than a top-down, structured method.

Best App for Editing Office Documents

Quickoffice Mobile Office Suite
$19.99
Version: 1.3
Quickoffice

Edit Microsoft Word and Excel files—and view a slew of other file types—with this capable suite for editing and sharing documents. It's actually three apps in one, or you can buy them one at a time: Quickword ($12.99) for Word docs; Quicksheet ($12.99) for spreadsheets; and Quickoffice Files ($1.99) for swapping files with other computers and online disks.

FILL UP ON FILES. Tap a .doc, .xls, or .txt file to edit, or tap other files for read-only viewing (PDF, PowerPoint, .docx, .xlsx, and others). Connect to MobileMe iDisks to copy files back and forth, or share files with other computers on the same WiFi network. Apps aren't allowed direct access to email attachments,, but Quickoffice sidesteps this limitation by providing a special email address where you can forward files for editing.

A KIND WORD: Quickword manages basic word processing without a hitch, letting you edit text and add formatting, including font styles and size. It's easy: Double-tap to highlight text, drag the blue handles to select, then choose the formatting you want. Although you can't *add* images or tables to documents, the app manages their display just fine for documents where they already exist.

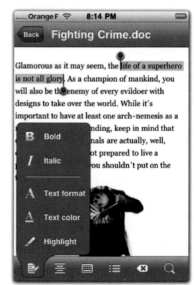

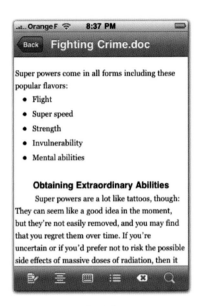

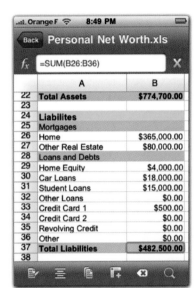

ON THE DOCK: Other dock icons manage text alignment, conjure the keyboard, create bullet lists, delete text, or search the document. To undo or redo the last action, you shake the iPhone to summon Quickword's undo/redo controls. You can browse and edit Word and text files in landscape view, too, although the formatting options aren't available in that view—only the keyboard.

GIMME A GRID: Quicksheet includes all the spreadsheet fundamentals, including 125 common formula functions, text and cell formatting, and control over row and column structure. Double-tap a cell to edit its contents, or double-tap-drag to select several cells to format or to copy and paste. Like Quickword, you can zoom in and out of documents by pinching the screen, browse and edit in landscape view, or shake to undo.

WORKSHEETS: Spreadsheets can contain multiple worksheets, and Quicksheet provides tools to add, delete, shuffle, and rename your worksheets. As with any spreadsheet program, you can apply calculations or look up cell values across worksheets.

Best App for Taking Notes

Evernote

Free
Version: 3.0.2
Evernote

Far more than a notepad, Evernote is a self-organizing file cabinet for all the info you care to keep. It's Google for your brain. Chuck anything into it, and Evernote's search finds it for you. It even reads text in photos; snap a business card or scribbled note, and fetch it later with a text search. Notes are stored at *evernote.com,* so you can also get at 'em on the Web or with free desktop software, where you can also add files to your personal archive.

WORTH A THOUSAND WORDS: Add text, photo, or voice notes. Photos are especially easy ways to grab info from menus, books, sticky notes, or museum wall text—Evernote recognizes and indexes any text or handwriting in your pictures. Alas, Evernote doesn't transcribe speech, but its voice memos are still convenient ways to leave yourself a reminder. Record up to ten minutes per note, and play them back when you're ready.

LEAVE THE MARKER AT HOME: Evernote does its work in business-like Helvetica instead of the funky Marker Felt font preferred by the built-in Notes app. You can also flip it on its side to edit in landscape view. Photos and recorded audio appear as attachments to a regular note; add descriptive text, or give it tags to add your own personal categories to the note. When you're done, the app saves the note in your *evernote.com* account.

WriteRoom

$4.99
Version: 2.0
Hog Bay Software

If all of Evernote's derring-do is more than you want in a notepad, WriteRoom offers a minimalist alternative well suited for collecting and sharing plain-text notes. Its austere white-on-black editor works in landscape and portrait views and includes a word count, too. WriteRoom syncs notes to the app's website, where you can access the text from any computer. You can also share files over a local WiFi network, allowing any computer on the same network to edit your notes live, effectively creating a remote keyboard for your iPhone.

HEAD IN THE CLOUD: You can browse the titles and thumbnails of all notes offline, but because the full contents of each note are stored online, you need Internet access to consult details except for recently viewed notes or those marked as favorites. Evernote lets you read attached documents, but with a catch: Free *evernote.com* accounts work only with PDF, images, and audio. Other file types require a paid account.

ON THE MAP: When you add a note from your iPhone, Evernote grabs your current location, too, letting you browse notes by location. When you pass a store you'd like to visit, add a note, and the map feature will help you find it later. Or photograph the label of a tasty wine at a restaurant and quickly look it up if you want to order the same wine next time. You can also search notes or browse them by date, title, city, or country.

19

Best App for Documents on the Go

ReaddleDocs

$4.99
Version: 1.5.2
Readdle

ReaddleDocs is the Rolls Royce of document portfolios. Lots of other apps (including Quickoffice and Evernote) let you share, store, and browse files, but this app offers the cleverest mix of methods to spirit files on and off your iPhone. It talks to popular online storage services (like MobileMe or Box.net), downloads from websites, exchanges with computers on the same network, and lets you email files back and forth.

DISK JOCKEY: Swap files with any online disk using WebDAV technology, including Readdle Storage, where you get 512MB of space and a special email address to send files to add to the disk. Also, computers on the same WiFi network can download your files via web browser or add your iPhone as a network disk to exchange documents. The app's built-in browser lets you grab files from the Web or other ReaddleDocs users.

FILE FRENZY: Organize files into folders, and open a wide range of file types for reading. The app can open any file iPhone supports, including Microsoft Word, Excel, PDF, and PowerPoint. Zip files work, too; here, opening Archive.zip created the Archive folder. ReaddleDocs makes for easy reading, too, letting you bookmark pages and scroll quickly through long documents. Pass files along to friends and coworkers via email.

At Work

Best App for Swapping Contacts

Mover

Free
Version: 1.0.2
Infinite Labs

Mover makes it easy to send contacts and photos with a flourish to other iPhones and iPods on the same WiFi network. The app shows the names of up to four others with Mover open on the same network, each staking out one side of the screen. Just flick a contact or photo toward the name of the iPhone you're sharing with, and it skids into view on the receiving end, automatically saved to that phone's contact list or camera roll.

CONTACT SHEET: Choose the photos or contacts to share, and Mover adds a slide for each one to your screen. (Sorry, as handy as it would be, you can't swap other info like calendar events, music, or notes.)

SLIDE THE SLIDES: When other iPhones or iPods on the same WiFi network open Mover, their names appear at the edges of the screen. No need to pair the devices or otherwise authenticate them; they just show up without a fuss. Flick a slide offscreen toward the name of the iPhone you're sending it to, and after a moment, it slides onto the screen of the other phone, where the contact or slide is saved.

Best App for Personal Databases

Bento

$4.99
Version: 1.0.1
Filemaker

Boil it down, and Bento is really an app for creating your own apps—a stash of flexible databases for any info you want organized. At work, it can manage sales leads or track your shop's inventory; at home, it's a recipe book, an exercise log, a catalog of your DVD collection, you name it. It's a solid app on its own, but it's at its best paired with Bento for Mac ($49), the only way to sync your iPhone database to one or more computers.

HEAD LIBRARIAN: Bento organizes its information into one or more databases, or "libraries" in Bentospeak. For every type of info you want to organize, you create a new library. The app gives you a headstart by offering a parade of 25 templates, prestocked with data fields for various common needs, from tracking billable hours or project milestones to homework assignments or diet details. Pick one, or start from a blank slate.

A LIBRARY FOR EVERY TOPIC: The Home screen shows all the libraries you've created in either a list view, shown here, or a slick carousel of icons (toggle between the two views by tapping the button at top left). Each of the libraries contains its own separate data, organized into different fields, but you can still search all of them at once by tapping the Search icon in the dock. Tap a specific library to browse, search, or edit its data.

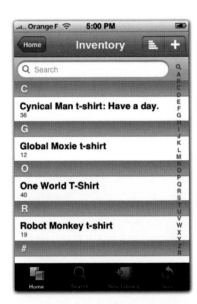

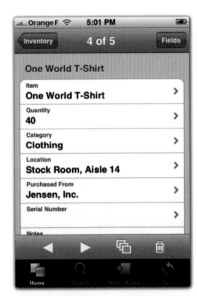

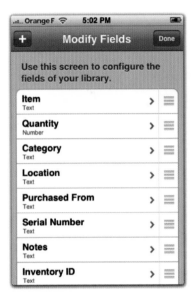

THE CONTACTS CONNECTION: Tap a library from the Home screen, and Bento shows its data with the same familiar organization as iPhone's Contacts app, with tappable shortcuts down the side for hopping around the alphabet. In fact, the big-picture concept of Bento libraries is very much like your address book. Each entry has its own data record, composed of several data fields. Tap a record to see its details, or tap + for a new entry.

THE NITTY-GRITTY: A record's detail screen shows all of its content, tidily organized into data fields. Tap a field to edit its contents, or use the arrows at the bottom of the screen to move back and forth through the library's records. Tap the three-card icon to assign the record to one or more "collections," a handy way to categorize records. Tap the Fields button to modify the database structure by adding, removing, or renaming fields.

OPEN FIELDS: The Modify Fields screen lets you customize your database, pruning fields you don't use and adding new ones. Use this screen to build a database from scratch or modify one of the template libraries. Tap the + button to add a new field, first telling Bento what type of data the field will hold (number, text, date, time, picture, and so on). When you're done, you've got an app that holds the precise info that's important to you.

Best App for Making Recordings

bottle rocket

Voxie Pro Recorder
$1.99
Version: 2.5
Bottle Rocket

Note to self: Voice memos are a fast way to capture big ideas and fleeting thoughts. Voxie distinguishes itself from the many apps that turn iPhones and iPods into dictaphones (including the built-in Voice Memos app) with its sleek interface, easy audio export, and a lightning-fast paid transcription service handled by actual human beings, including specialists in legal lingo. Record clips of any length in your choice of four quality levels.

SPEAK EASY: Voxie lets you pause and resume recordings. During playback, skip to any part of the clip by tapping the progress bar at the bottom of the screen. File your recordings in custom categories, and email them to yourself or others. Any computer on the same WiFi network can also download the audio files via web browser. File sizes vary according to your chosen quality level; basic voice memos run about 1MB per minute.

TALK FAST: "Express mode" dispenses with all the buttons. Tap the screen or shake to start and stop. Set preferences to save or email these express recordings automatically. Want that in writing? Voxie's paid audio transcription offers fast, accurate turnaround in just a few minutes by honest-to-god typists. The app comes with a free 100-word trial (about a minute of speech); after that, monthly plans start at $5 for 200 words/month.

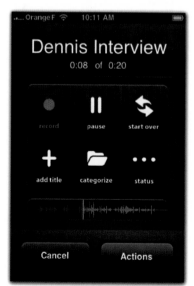

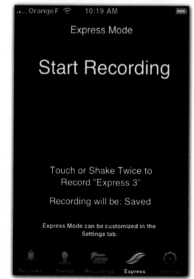

Best App for Printing from iPhone

Print n Share

$6.99
Version: 3.2.1
EuroSmartz

Liberate contacts, webpages, email, photos, and documents from your tiny touchscreen and onto the printed page. With the help of free software installed on your Mac or PC, Print & Share can talk to any printer connected to that computer when you're on the same WiFi network—or even, conditions permitting, from anywhere on the Internet. The app doubles as a document briefcase, letting you swap and read files from your computer.

HARD COPY: Choose what to print from the main screen. iPhone limitations don't let apps get direct access to the Mobile Safari or Mail apps, so Print & Share has its own browser and email programs, which you must use to print webpages or email messages. You can also exchange files with the same computer that you use to print. Save files on your iPhone to print or read later, and share them with others via email.

PAPER TIGER: Select the stuff to commit to paper, and Print & Share searches the network to find a computer with the companion WePrint software installed. If you're not on the same WiFi network but you know the computer's Internet address, just type it in to connect from anywhere in the world, firewalls allowing. Select your printer, and send your files, contacts, pictures, and webpages on their way.

Best App for Free and Cheap Calls

Skype

Free
Version: 1.1
Skype Software

Put Skype's popular Internet phone-calling service on your iPhone to make free or dirt-cheap calls to anyone in the world when you're connected to a WiFi network. Skype calls don't count against your regular cellphone minutes, so you can stretch your phone time at very little cost. Call other Skype users for free, or dial regular phones for a modest fee. Turn your iPod Touch into a phone, too, with a microphone headset.

CALL LIST: Browse or edit Skype users or regular phone numbers in your Skype account's contact list. View them all at once or tap the Online button to see only those currently signed into Skype—those are the folks you can call or chat with for free. Icons show whether contacts are away, accepting calls, or busy. Tap a contact to call her, start a text chat, or view her profile, where you can also add a profile photo with your iPhone camera.

BY THE NUMBERS: Call anyone you want, anywhere in the world. Punch the number into the dial pad, or tap the address book icon to pick a number from your iPhone contacts. Dialing a number instead of another Skype account does cost some coin, but those coins are usually pennies. Check *skype.com* for rates. To make calls, you first have to add credit to your account balance, which you can purchase from the My Info screen.

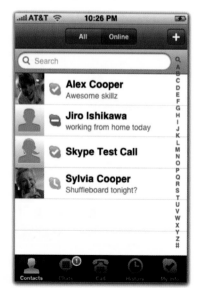

At Work

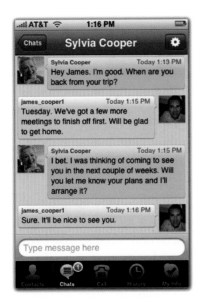

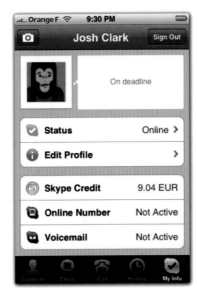

SPEECH BUBBLES: Fire up free instant-message text chats with other Skype users. You can run multiple conversations at once, and the Chats icon shows your count of active chats. You can skip running a comb through your hair beforehand: While video chat is a staple of Skype's desktop software, it's not available for iPhone. Your friends and coworkers see only your profile picture and, of course, your clever commentary.

YOUR 411: Tap My Info to update your status, mood message, and profile details. Add or change your profile photo by snapping a new photo with the iPhone camera or choosing from your photo library. This control panel also lets you check and refill your balance, buy a local phone number to let others call your Skype account from regular phones, or add voicemail to take messages when you're not online or answering calls.

The Skinny on Skype

Skype is a bonafide marvel, but it's not a complete phone replacement. In particular, don't expect to use Skype everywhere you go. Your phone company won't let the app make calls over its Edge or 3G mobile networks, so you can talk only when you're on WiFi. (You can do text chats anywhere, though.)

Also, while Skype for iPhone is terrific for making calls, it's less useful for *receiving* them. You can catch Skype calls and chats only when the app is running front and center. If you switch to a different app, Skype quits—a limitation of the iPhone itself—and it can't accept calls. To other Skype users, it looks like you're offline. For a fee, though, you can add voicemail to your account so that callers can leave voicemail while you're busy playing that video game.

Best App for Reaching a Human Being

Dial Zero
Free
Version: 1.7
Next Mobile Web

"If you can't stand this voicemail system, press or say one." When calls to customer-service numbers get lost in a maze of touch-tone prompts and greetings from recorded robots, Dial Zero helps you find a human voice. The app lists the toll-free numbers of hundreds of companies—that alone is useful—but also offers the precise steps for reaching a human operator.

LIVE AND IN PERSON: Tap the name of a company to get its customer-service number along with instructions for sidestepping the answering system. Tap the number to dial. The app also includes "tips" from other callers, a good idea that unfortunately disintegrates under the pressure of human nature. While the comments are occasionally useful, most are rants about the specific company or adolescent pull-my-finger graffiti.

HONORABLE MENTION

Direct Line
$0.99
Version: 3
Michael Schneider / Hive Brain

Like Dial Zero, Direct Line collects customer-service numbers for a huge list of companies. The list on offer is smaller than Dial Zero's but the app handles the keypress combinations for you. Tap a company name and Direct Line makes the call, pausing and pressing at all the right times in the voicemail dance to weave its way to an operator. The app doesn't offer community comments like Dial Zero, but in most cases that turns out to be a strength, not a weakness.

At Work

Best App for Voice Dialing

Vlingo

Free
Version: 1.0.3
Vlingo Corporation

iPhone 3GS phones come with voice dialing, but older models remain speechless. Vlingo gives voice to those phones, too. Stop fumbling with your contact list and just tell Vlingo who to call. Say, "Call Gunther at home," and the app does it. Got multiple Gunthers in your life? Vlingo shows the options; tap the lucky Gunther to call. The app also lets you speak web searches, Facebook and Twitter updates, or map requests.

SAY WHAT YOU WANT: Fire off a variety of voice commands from the Home screen. Place a call to anyone in your address book ("Call Jeffrey Lebowski"), search the Web ("Google: body odor solutions"), map addresses or services ("Find pizza"), or update your online profile ("Facebook: is waiting for pizza"). Vlingo's voice recognition isn't quite as good as Google Mobile for searches, but it's quite good at recognizing contacts to dial.

PUT ME THROUGH, OPERATOR: Under the app's standard settings, Vlingo dials numbers automatically after a brief delay. You can adjust the amount of delay, or turn auto-dialing off entirely if you prefer to tap a number to start the call. For contacts with more than one number, just say which one you want: "Call Captain Fantastic on his mobile."

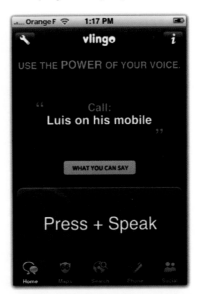

Best Remote Control

Air Mouse Pro
$5.99
Version: 1.5.4
RPA Tech

Turn your iPhone or iPod Touch into a mouse, keyboard, and remote control for your PC or Mac, a boon for stage-stalking presenters or couch-happy movie watchers. Along with free software that you install on your WiFi-connected computer, Air Mouse Pro steers the cursor like a laser pointer or trackpad; its keyboard does the typing. The app morphs based on what's on-screen, so you get playback controls when you use iTunes, for example.

MIGHTY MOUSE: The trackpad controls your computer's cursor, along with left- and right-click buttons and a scroll wheel (the orange arrows) that thumbs through the active window. The keyboard lets you type onscreen as you'd expect. Switch to "mouse" mode to use the app like a laser pointer, moving the cursor as you wave your iPhone in the air. Tapping the arrows at top right switches between trackpad and mouse mode.

Tip: Looking for a simpler remote just for audio and video? See page 118.

MEDIA-SAVVY: The app knows when you're working with an audio or video program on your computer, showing playback buttons for easy control of movies and music.

At Work

FUNCTION FUN: The function screen gives you access to arrow and function keys, as well as a handy set of "hot keys" that you can configure to run your favorite desktop programs or type a keyboard shortcut.

 HONORABLE MENTION

Keynote Remote
$0.99
Version: 1.1
Apple

Free yourself from the podium when giving a slideshow presentation. If you use Apple's Keynote presentation software (part of the company's iWork productivity suite), Keynote Remote lets you drive slideshows with your iPhone or iPod Touch. Flick to the next slide on your handheld screen, and the slide changes on the big screen, too. More than just a clicker, the app lets you see your presenter notes for the current slide or preview the next slide—a presentation cheatsheet in the palm of your hand. *Requires iWork '09 and a WiFi network.*

SLIDESHOW WRANGLER: Keynote Remote gives you a choice of two slideshow views. Here, the portrait view shows you the presenter notes for the current slide. Choose landscape view to show both the current slide and a preview of the next slide (but no presenter notes). Flick the slides left or right to move back and forth in your presentation, or tap the Options button to skip to the first or last slide.

Best App for Desktop Remote Access

Jaadu VNC
$24.99
Version: 3.0
Jugaari

Jaadu puts your entire desktop on your iPhone or iPod Touch, working your computer when it's on the same WiFi network—or across the Internet, with a bit of network know-how. After some modest setup on your computer (it's a snap on Macs, slightly more involved on PCs), you can do anything from your iPhone that you could at your keyboard. It's pricey, but it buys complete access to your computer from anywhere in the world.

JUMP RIGHT IN: Choose a computer to connect to, and Jaadu teleports you in with a nifty blue spinning wormhole effect that reveals your desktop. Pinch to zoom in and out, and use the touchscreen to move the cursor around the screen, tapping to click.

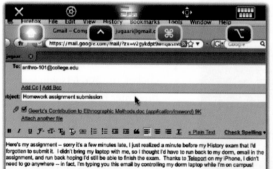

REMOTE POSSIBILITY: Browse files and use your computer just like you would if you were sitting in front of it. Tap the keyboard icon to type email or do some remote word-processing. Control your desktop in either landscape or portrait view.

32

Best App for Personal Web Stats

Ego

$1.99
Version: 1.4
Garrett Murray

Are you Internet famous? Monitor the health of your online popularity with this compact, at-a-glance dashboard of personal online stats. Track the number of visits to your website, subscribers to your site's news feed, or the Twitter followers you've won over. Ego also monitors your site's authority with Google, showing the PageRank for specific web pages. If you measure your self-worth in page hits, Ego is the app for you.

WHIP UP YOUR WIDGETS: Build your collection of stats by adding "widgets" to your Ego dashboard. Each widget contacts an online service for info about your site or Twitter account. Ego offers widgets to track RSS subscribers via FeedBurner; web traffic via Google Analytics, Mint, or Squarespace; Google PageRank; and Twitter followers. Most of these services are free but require you to set up an account to start tracking stats.

EGO BOOST: After setting up your website and Twitter widgets, Ego fetches and displays the stats for each widget. Tap a web-traffic widget to switch among counts for daily, hourly, monthly, and yearly visits. You can add widgets for as many sites or Twitter accounts as you like, great for monitoring both personal and work sites, for example.

33

Best App for Unit Conversions

Convertbot
$0.99
Version: 1.3.1
Tapbots

Don't speak metric? Got a yen for foreign currencies? Convertbot helps you convert units of all kinds with a stylish interface that dials up the answer to your conversion conundrum. Convertbot handles currency, length, mass, volume, area, temperature, and many other conversions, over 400 units in all. This clever little bot can even manage mixed units: Give it lengths in feet and inches, for example, or weights in pounds and ounces.

TOUCH THAT DIAL: Spin Convertbot's dial to choose the type of conversion you're after. The bottom of the dial shows the units you're working with. Here, the mass icon is selected, and the units are set to do a conversion from pounds and ounces to kilograms. Tap one of the units to switch to a different unit, or tap the center button to convert in the other direction.

DO THE MATH: Tap the display screen at the top, and the dial slides away to reveal the keypad. Type the "from" value, and Convertbot shows you the converted value.

Best App for Scientific Calculations

PCalc RPN Calculator

Free lite version / $9.99 full version
Version: 1.7
TLA Systems

Your iPhone or iPod comes with its own capable calculator; turn it on its side, and it even knows trigonometry. But when you need more hardcore scientific or engineering functions, turn to PCalc. It includes an optional two-line display, multiple undo and redo, unit conversions, quick lookup of common constants, support for binary, octal, and hexadecimal number systems, and (believe it or not) much more. PCalc handles all the math you can muster.

HOT NUMBER: Flip PCalc on its side to see more functions (the portrait view shows a simple traditional calculator). Tap the 2nd button to see the app's trig and log functions. Tap 42 to insert constants, tap Tape to view your history, or tap AB to do unit conversions. You can even change the calculator's look and sound with custom skins.

Astronomical	
Equatorial Radius Of Earth	6378 km
Equatorial Radius Of Sun	6.955e5 km
Mass Of Earth	5.974e24 kg
Mass Of Moon	7.348e22 kg
Mass Of Sun	1.989e30 kg

DEATH AND TAXES: Many things are constant in life, especially in science and math. PCalc offers an easy way to insert common constants into your calculations, all of them organized into topical categories. Tap the constant to add its value to the calculator's digital display.

Best Apps on the Town

Put on your glad rags for a night on the town, and make your iPhone the primary accessory. Loaded with the right apps, the iPhone and iPod Touch are savvy sources of info—connoisseurs of fine food *and* masters of ceremonies for upcoming local events. Even better, your iPhone's built-in GPS makes it the perfect scout for finding the closest good time or nearby friends.

This chapter tours the best apps for going out. For an evening of **wining and dining,** your iPhone can recommend the best nearby restaurants—and even make a reservation automatically without so much as a whisper to the maître d'. Why stop at restaurants? When you're wondering **what's nearby,** a bevy of apps are at the ready to give you the lowdown on any local shop or service, with reviews and ratings from other customers. That goes for **the silver screen,** too; you'll discover the best apps for grabbing movie tickets and show times in a flash, including a sneak preview of reviews and trailers. If you have a more high-brow outing in mind, other apps are great for **soaking up culture,** from finding art exhibitions to live music.

Put it all together, and your iPhone is suddenly the perfect sidekick for any excursion—informed and ready for fun. (It might even make your date jealous.)

Photo: Luis Munoz-Najar/luismuna.com

Best App for Picking a Restaurant

Urbanspoon

Free
Version: 1.10
Urbanspoon.com

Shake up your dining routine (literally) and discover new tables in your city. Give your iPhone or iPod Touch a shake, and this app's wheels whir to provide a random restaurant pick, complete with reviews and user votes. Zero in on a neighborhood, cuisine, or price range—or put randomness aside and search for specifics, browse by category, or see friends' favorites. The app covers towns and cities in the US, Canada, UK, and Australia.

FEELING LUCKY? Urbanspoon's slot machine turns choosing a restaurant into a game of chance. Set the wheels in motion by shaking your iPhone (or tap Shake if you're not feeling vigorous). When the wheels for neighborhood, cuisine, and price stop spinning, the app spits out a restaurant to match. Shake again for another suggestion. To narrow the types of restaurant, lock one or more wheels on a specific setting.

THE SKINNY: Get the scoop on a resto by tapping its name on the slot-machine screen. The summary screen shows the thumbs-up count from other Urbanspoon users and let's you add your vote, too. Tap the phone number to call, or tap the address to map the location. The Save button offers options to add the restaurant to your Urbanspoon favorites or wishlist, or to email it, Twitter it, or add its entry to the Contacts app.

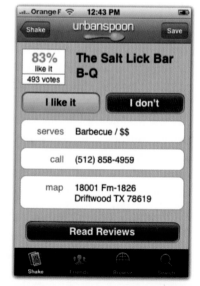

THE CHATTER: Tap the Read Reviews button on the summary screen to conjure the restaurant's detail screen, which includes menus and brief reviews from newspapers, websites, blogs, and other Urbanspoon users. Click any summary to see the full text in Urbanspoon's built-in web browser.

A LA CARTE: Also on a restaurant's detail screen: Tap the "View the Menu" button to find out what's on offer. Menus are provided by Urbanspoon users, and not all restaurants have menus. When that's the case, the app offers to let you add a menu with your iPhone's camera. (Sorry, that option's not available for iPod Touch.)

DISH YOUR EXPERIENCE: Add your own review to the mix. Tap the "Write a Review" button on the restaurant's reviews screen to reveal a brief form. After submitting your tasteful commentary, your review appears on the restaurant's detail screen. If you use Twitter (page 64), you can give Urbanspoon your account details and automatically post your review as a tweet, too.

Other Apps for Picking a Restaurant

 **HONORABLE MENTION**

Zagat To Go '09
$9.99
Version: 2.1.001
Handmark

 **HONORABLE MENTION**

VegOut
$2.99
Version: 1.1
Front-Ended

This "venerable restaurant guide" has long been an "indispensable resource" for capsule dining reviews. While most say Zagat's "simple, reliable snapshots" of area restaurants make its guides a "must have for local foodies," others note that it's "a little thin" in smaller cities.

This recipe is familiar to anyone who's ever cracked a Zagat city guide for its quick reviews based on diners' quotes, and it makes for a tasty iPhone app. Explore local restaurants by category, cuisine, or feature (outdoor dining, brunch, and so on) then sort by rating, price, or proximity—a nifty use of your iPhone's GPS. You get access to over 40,000 listings, and it's deep for big cities, including international hotspots like Paris or Tokyo, but don't expect to find lots in smaller cities (only two restaurants for all of Idaho, one of them a Cheesecake Factory). The app refreshes its review info online but only through the end of the year, when you have to buy a new edition to get the latest info.

If you're anxiously in search of a vegetarian restaurant either at home or on the road, don't have a cow. Consult VegOut, a remarkably thorough catalog of vegetarian eateries. The app gets its listings from *HappyCow.net*, an international community of vegan and vegetarian foodies with a deep archive of restaurant info and reviews in cities around the world.

The app's standard settings use your iPhone's GPS to show the restaurants closest to your current location, but you can also choose to find locations near any location you like, useful when making travel plans. The app flags each entry as vegan, vegetarian, or vegetarian-friendly and lets you sort results by location, rating, or name. Tap a restaurant to see its details, including customer reviews at *HappyCow.net*. VegOut also lets you visualize your veggies by showing all of the nearby restaurant locations in the Maps app.

Best App for Reserving a Table

OpenTable

Free
Version: 1.1.3
OpenTable

OpenTable is a reservation service for booking tables at participating restaurants. The app finds places in most US states and several international cities, but it's at its best in the biggest cities where lots of restaurants have signed up. Tell OpenTable when you want to eat, and it shows you all the restaurants with availability. Search by neighborhood, or only the restaurants closest to your current location. Pick a spot, and the app holds your table.

ON THE RESERVATION: The app searches for the 100 closest restaurants with an open table, or you can select a specific city and neighborhood to search, as shown here. Choose a date and time, add the number of people in your group, and OpenTable finds restaurants with availability within a two-hour window of the requested time. You can further filter results by cuisine, price, or restaurant name.

DINING DETAILS: Choose the restaurant where you want to eat, and OpenTable shows you additional details, including the restaurant's menu and a photo of the dining room. Tap the time you'd like to book, provide your personal info, and you're done. The app also offers to email the reservation confirmation details to your hungry dining companions.

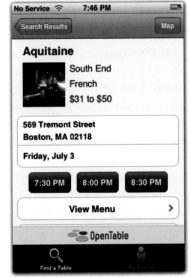

Best App for Selecting a Wine

Wine Steward

$0.99
Version: 1.1
Inkling Technology Partners

Don't know syrah from sangiovese? Wine Steward helps you out, suggesting wines to match what you're eating. The app knows an astounding number of dishes, offering wine pairings for food as varied as beef wellington, orange cuttlefish, bread pudding, or bacon and eggs. It doesn't recommend specific wines, but rather the *type* of wine. It points you to the right page of the wine list, in other words, and you take it from there.

WHAT'S ON THE MENU? Tell Wine Steward what you're eating, and it suggests several wines to try, along with a percentage rating showing the app's confidence. Wine pairings are very literally a matter of taste, of course, and the app reveals a decided preference for pinots, but even when the top pick isn't what you're in the mood for, one of the other suggestions will almost certainly point you in the right direction.

WINE WISDOM: Tap a wine to get a description of the grape or region. Some of the entries are brief, like the pinot gris entry shown here, while others are practically essay-length dissertations. Tap a star at the bottom of the screen to rate the suggestion and help improve pairings.

TASTE TESTER: The Personalize screen asks questions about your tastes to help tailor suggestions to your wine preferences. Questions vary from the practical ("Do you like finding wine bargains?") to more abstract matters of flavor ("Cherries or plums?").

WINE JOURNAL: After you've drained your bottle, jot down your thoughts about the wine in the app's journal to help remember the hits and misses. You can add photos of wine labels, too, which triggers a fun browsing feature in the app: Turn your iPhone or iPod Touch on its side to browse your wines by label, just like you can browse album covers in the built-in iPod app.

WINES OF THE WORLD: See what food and wine others are trying around the world. Pairings and wines bubble up from the planet's surface as someone in Chicago has a steak and zinfandel while a Californian samples sushi and champagne (your own pairings and location show up, too). OK, so it might not be wildly useful, but the feature is oddly hypnotic and helps inspire food and wine pairings you might not have considered.

Other Apps for Selecting a Wine

Cellar Rat

$2.99
Version: 1.01
WineVintageCard.com

Cellar Rat scurries into the wine roundup with a simple but useful crib sheet to tell you how various wine regions fare for specific vintages. Whip out your iPhone or iPod Touch when you're at the wine shop or browsing the wine list to see whether 1998 was a good year for Napa Valley (it wasn't), or whether you should instead try a 1999 bottle from Oregon's Wilamette Valley (yes!). Cellar Rat rates over 60 regions worldwide for wines since 1990 with a quick at-a-glance format.

WINE HAPPY: Cellar Rat's cute icons indicate whether a region's wines are worth trying for specific vintages. A toothy grin tells you it's a must-buy, while a green Mr. Yuk suggests that you pass it by. The app's two screens organize regions by Europe and everywhere else. Swipe up and down to see more regions, or left and right to see more years. Flip it on its side for landscape view.

Cor.kz Wine Info

$4.99
Version: 2.0.2
Applied Ambiguities

Cor.kz is a vast, detailed wine reference, with online access to *cellartracker.com* and its database of more than half a million wines, including nearly a million reviews contributed by the site's community of wine enthusiasts. Search for wines to see details, ratings, and reviews for specific vintages, and use the app to track your personal wine collection and tasting sessions. The app will likely overwhelm wine novices but provides a terrific resource for serious wine geeks.

Best App for Mixing Cocktails

Cocktails+

$2.99
Version: 1.6.2
Skorpiostech

This carefully crafted encyclopedia of liquid wisdom provides recipes for over 2000 classic and contemporary cocktails. Other cocktail apps might provide more recipes, but Cocktails+ gets the nod for its evident attention to the selection of potions, even providing multiple recipes that track the history of some drinks back into the 19th century. Whether you're a master mixologist or a cocktail dilettante, this is your behind-the-bar handbook.

POTENT POTABLES: The Browse screen organizes drinks like your iPhone contacts, letting you browse alphabetically or search by name or ingredient. Every drink shows a silhouette of the proper glass to use for serving, along with a brief list of the contents. You can also browse drinks by base liquor, drink type, flavor (anise, apple, and apricot!), or tag category.

COCKTAIL HISTORIAN: Tap a cocktail to see its recipe. Many classic cocktails have several recipes, each dated and footnoted with its original source. As you go back in time, recipes age, like this 1930 gem for the Manhattan cocktail. Tap an ingredient for background info and substitution suggestions if you don't have an element on hand. Tap the star icon to save the cocktail to your favorites list for future reference.

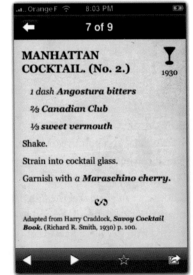

Best App for Local Recommendations

Yelp

Free
Version: 2.0.2
Yelp

Yelp.com is the kingpin of grassroots review resources, featuring 6 million reviews of businesses across the US, Canada, the UK, and Ireland. Let the site's official app point you to a great bite, a spirited watering hole, a reliable oil change, or a brainy bookstore. Choose a category, and the app lists nearby businesses, ranked and reviewed by a gaggle of irreverent (and voluble) yelpers. Find what's popular, or add your own voice to the mix.

BURSTING WITH BUSINESSES: Yelp gets you started with a selection of popular categories. Make a selection, and Yelp lists the businesses closest to you. Restaurants, bars, and coffee shops headline the category list (and earn the vast majority of reviews), but Yelp offers ratings for just about any service you might need, from acupuncture to veterinarians.

RATED RESULTS: When you've got something specific in mind, tap the Search icon and enter a business name or keyword. Like the category search, Yelp lists matches by proximity and shows the address, rating, and number of reviews for each. Tap the Filter button to winnow results by price or opening hours, or tap the Map button to see the results pinned down around you.

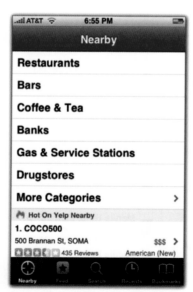

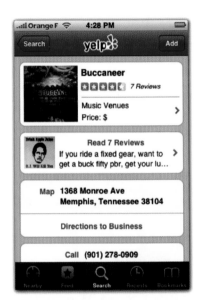

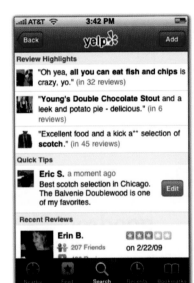

DIRECTORY DETAILS: Yelp offers to map, call, or give directions for any of its listings, which just on its own makes for a useful resource. Yelp's big draw, though, is its deep collection of tell-it-like-it-is reviews from local customers. The business page shows a snippet from one review; tap for more, or contribute your own quick tip, add a photo, or start drafting a longer review.

LOCAL COLOR: Yelp's listings feature wall-to-wall commentary, with popular venues running to hundreds of impassioned reviews. (Entire dissertations have been written on why a Chinese restaurant's kung pao chicken deserves three stars instead of four.) The app keeps this manageable by capping the display at 50 reviews, featuring shorter "quick tips," and highlighting reviews that include popular terms or phrases for the business.

DISH YOUR EXPERIENCE: Yelp encourages you to add your two cents, too—but not a penny more. The app accepts only short, Twitter-style quick tips of 140 characters or less. The app lets you draft longer reviews, but you can publish those from the website only, not the app itself. Either way, you'll need a free *Yelp.com* account to share your wisdom. An account also lets you bookmark listings and track friends' reviews.

Another App for Local Recommendations

➕ **HONORABLE MENTION**

Goodrec

Free
Version: 1.0.6
Goodrec

Like Yelp, Goodrec helps you find reliable businesses with the help of friends and other locals, but it reviews other stuff, too, including wine, movies, and books. Browse only your friends' opinions, or open yourself to the notions of the masses. Cast your own thumbs-up/thumbs-down votes, and post quick reviews of 160 characters or less. Goodrec doesn't yet have the same following as Yelp, but it's available in cities around the world.

FEELING LUCKY? Tap the Search icon to tell Goodrec what you're looking for. Swipe through the big glossy icons at the bottom of the screen, and tap to find recommendations for bars, restaurants, movies, books, wines, products, or local services. Use your current location or any other place, and Goodrec shows you the closest addresses when searching for businesses.

ON THE MAP: Goodrec maps its finds around your location. Pinch to zoom in or out; as you get closer to the ground, more results materialize. Tap a pin to see the business name and its thumbs-up and thumbs-down votes in green and red. You can short-circuit these visual niceties by tapping the List button to scan through a text display instead. Either way, Tap the name to see reviews or cast your own vote.

On the Town

48

Best App for Finding Your Friends

Loopt

Free
Version: 1.7
Loopt

Discover the capers and coordinates of your whole crew at a glance. Loopt lets you and your pals announce where you are and what you're doing, a convenient way to hook up with friends when you're on the prowl—or a vaguely creepy way to keep tabs on others. It's up to you! The app's privacy settings let you choose when and how others can find you. You can share Loopt updates and location info via Twitter and Facebook, too.

SOCIAL MAP: The map shows your location in red and your friends in blue. Tap a marker to show a friend's current status, review their journal, send a text, or call. To see everyone's status at once, tap the Friends icon in the dock to dismiss the map and get a list view. You can also add businesses to the mix; the Search icon summons a search of Yelp-powered reviews for the area. Post updates and photos by tapping the Share icon.

FRIENDS YOU'VE YET TO MEET: If you're looking to meet someone new—like *anyone*—turn on the Mix feature to share a limited profile with anyone nearby. Flag yourself as all business ("networking"), innocent fun ("friendship") or ready for love ("dating"). Exchange messages with your newfound friend from down the block in safe anonymity; they don't get your full name or contact info until you decide to share.

Best App for Sharing Your Adventures

Whrrl

Free
Version: 2.1
Pelago

Turn your outing—or anything you do—into a slideshow to share with others. Whrrl bundles photos and text messages into "stories." Friends can add to the tale from their phones, too. Anything's fair game: Your kid's birthday, a paintball match, a night out, a conference, whatever. Take photos, post messages, and when you're done, sign into *whrrl.com* to edit your story into a slideshow to share on the Web, on Facebook, or on Twitter.

STORYTELLERS: Whrrl's main screen shows a rundown of "featured stories": a mix of slideshows posted by you and your friends, along with publicly shared slideshows selected for greatness by the Whrrl staff. Tap a story to see the slideshow, or start your own by tapping "Say where you are." Announcing your location creates a new story where you post photos and messages.

LOCATION, LOCATION, LOCATION: Stories are pegged to places. If other Whrrl-toting friends are in the same place, they can join the story and add their own photos and messages. You control who can see the story as it's happening, changing the privacy settings anytime. You might share the story with more people, for example, after you get home and edit it into shape. The story ends when everyone leaves the location.

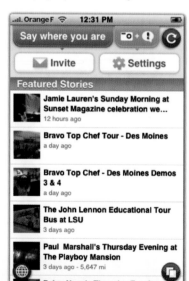

On the Town

FEED ME: Stories have two layouts, "feed view" and "story view." Feed view shows the blow-by-blow events that construct the story, listing the messages, photos, arrivals, departures, and comments that float through the location as the story happens. In either view, visitors can add a comment by tapping the speech-bubble icon next to messages and photos. Tap a profile photo to see more about a person, including their stories.

STORY VIEW: This is the slideshow of the event. Photos and messages are each individual slides; the effect is like a silent movie where images and dialogue weave together. The front "card" shows who was there as well as visitor comments. When you're done making the story, the slideshow remains on the Web, and you can edit it, share it, keep it private, or toss it out.

SHARE WITH ANYONE: Friends, family, and coworkers don't have to use Whrrl in order to see your adventures. Post stories on Facebook or Twitter while they're in progress. (After a story is finished, you can still share it, but you have to do it from the website.) You can also have Whrrl create a photo album on Facebook for every story you create, copying your story photos automatically to your Facebook account.

Best App for Finding Your Parked Car

Park'n Find

$1.99
Version: 1.0.1
Affinicore

You might think that an app like this would rely on the iPhone's GPS, but the gang behind Park'n Find knew better. (The phone's imprecise GPS could land you several aisles away, and it offers no help in parking garages.) Instead, this simple but reliable little app is a highly specialized notepad, enabling fast entry for parking details, including photos and audio notes to make sure you never misplace your ride again.

VALET PARKING: Park'n Find offers several methods to leave yourself breadcrumbs back to your parking space. Use as many or as few as you like: Fill in level, section, row, or spot numbers, take photos, or record a voice note. Once saved, the screen shows the elapsed time since you parked, convenient math for tracking the meter or fees for long-term parking.

TWO-CAR GARAGE: The app lets you save multiple parking spaces, which might be useful when you leave a car at the airport and pick up a rental on the other side. Tap a location to see its details, or tap Edit to clean up the list after you've finally found your car.

Best App for When You Can't Hold It

SitOrSquat

Free
Version: 3.0
Densebrain

When nature calls, it's SitOrSquat to the rescue. The database of public restrooms steers you to the closest porcelain oasis, including photos and ratings from a network of concerned citizens. That includes you: Update listings with photos, store hours, and ratings, or add new toilets as you explore your town's powder rooms. A blog of toilet humor provides bathroom reading, too. It's a full-service porta-potty for your mobile phone.

RESTROOM RADAR: SitOrSquat's map shows you the closest points of relief. Green and red icons indicate open and closed businesses (yellow means the database doesn't have that info). Select a business to see complete details, including photos, comments, and whether the facilities are clean ("sit") or dirty ("squat").

PORCELAIN OASIS: The Search screen shows results in list view, including photos, ratings and distance from your current location. Type a new location in the search box to find restrooms for another place, or filter results for cleanliness, business type, or a remarkable number of "features" (changing tables, handicap access, seat covers).

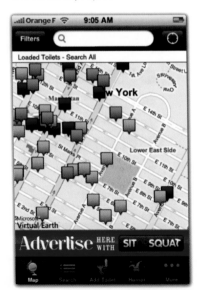

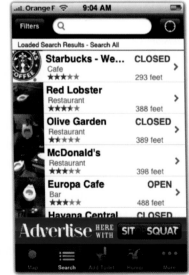

Best App for Movie Lovers

Now Playing

Free
Version: 3.8
Cyrus Najmabadi

The only thing missing from this full-featured movie app is the popcorn. Now Playing lists every movie on screens in your area, complete with trailers and a huge collection of published movie reviews. Scan films by release date and rating score, or browse by theater. The app lists showtimes and, in many cases, lets you buy tickets. Staying home? Browse new DVD releases, or use the app to manage your Netflix queue.

IN THEATERS NOW: The Movies screen shows all the films playing nearby, with the most recent releases topping the list. Each movie shows its ratings score from review site Rotten Tomatoes for a quick idea of how it's going down with critics. Check the coming attractions by tapping the Upcoming icon in the dock. The search option lets you find a specific film, but only if it's playing in your area.

FEATURED ATTRACTION: Every movie's detail screen has a brief summary, and most offer a trailer, too; the video is high-quality and quick to load. Tap the thumbnail image to see a full-screen version of the poster and, if you like, to save it in your photo library. Scroll down for theaters and showtimes, or tap "E-mail listings" to send the full rundown to friends. Tap the rating and running time to show the director and cast leads.

On the Town

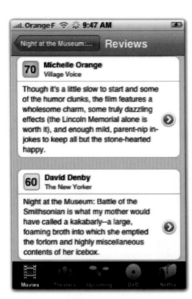

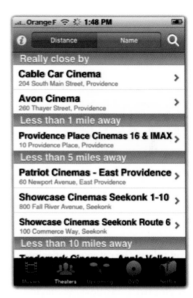

WHAT THE CRITICS SAY: Is the movie a stinker or an Oscar contender? Now Playing scours newspapers and magazines to furnish a large collection of published reviews for every movie. The list starts with the most positive reviews before shifting to crankier reactions as you move down the screen. Tap a review to read the full text in the app's built-in web browser.

ON SCREEN AND ONLINE: If this jumbo fountain drink of info still somehow leaves you thirsty, head to the Web to slurp down even more. Every movie offers a Websites button which reveals links to the movie's page at five popular sites.

MOVIEHOUSE MATCH-UPS: The Theaters screen shows you the closest theaters, sorted by either distance or name. Tap a theater to see the films and showtimes on offer. Settings let you change your location and choose how far the app should search for theaters. Now Playing has listings for cities around the world, so you can find out what's playing in the Paris movie houses before you jet over.

Another App for Movie Lovers

⊕ HONORABLE MENTION

Movies

Free
Version: 2.5
Flixster

This app nabs the prize for best supporting role in the category, offering many of Now Playing's features but with a plot twist. While Now Playing makes it easier to find local movies by limiting the view to films in your area, Movies aims to provide details on nearly every movie ever made, giving you a sprawling film encyclopedia. Hook it up to Facebook to share personal reviews and see what your friends are watching.

SCREEN PLAY: Browse current movies by popularity (box office sales) or rating, or use the search feature to find info, reviews, and trailers for thousands of other films and DVDs. Every movie listing includes a plot summary, along with reviews by professional critics as well as regular folks with Flixster accounts. Tap the Showtimes tab to find nearby theaters (US only) screening the film. In some cases, the app lets you buy tickets, too.

YOU'RE THE REVIEWER: Flixster is the engine behind the Movies app, an online community of average-Joe movie fans who rate and review films. The service is popular on Facebook, and when you connect the app to a Facebook account, you can post your own reviews of movies and DVDs, and browse your friends' opinions, too.

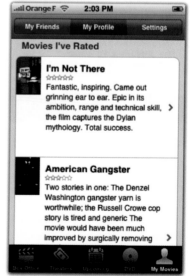

On the Town

Best App for Buying Movie Tickets

Moviefone

Free
Version: 1.1.2.8
AOL

"Hello, and welcome to Moviefone!" The iPhone version of the popular service skips its familiar greeting but provides a sleek, efficient way to get tickets from participating theaters. Browse films and theaters near you, or any US location you specify. When you find the theater you want, the app offers to email friends the showtimes before launching Safari to buy online.

GOAL IN SIGHT: In addition to showtimes, the app offers trailers and movie stills. Tap actors' names to see bios, photos, and a rundown of all their films. You can add celebrities and theaters to your list of favorites for quick access to listings for related films. When you're ready to buy your tickets, Moviefone hands you over to the Safari browser instead of handling the transaction itself, the only bump in an otherwise efficient process.

Fandango

Free
Version: 1.1
Fandango

Like Moviefone, Fandango sells tickets only for theaters that use its service. Most services use one or the other, so it's not a bad idea to have both these free apps in your collection to give you full coverage. Fandango has a slightly slower interface than Moviefone and lacks that app's photo extras, but it does offer some timesavers: You can make the purchase without going to a website, and the app offers to remember your credit card number for future reference and fewer taps.

Best App for Art Smarties

Artnear Pro

Free lite version / $4.99 pro
Version: 1.3
Hopnear

Quick, it's an art emergency! When you're struck by the sudden urge to admire some art, this global guide to the art world shepherds you to the closest venue. Artnear Pro includes an enormous address book of museums, galleries, artist residences, and other artsy destinations in medium and large cities around the world. Browse by proximity, or find results in the city of your choice. The app's calendar shows events and openings.

WHAT'S ON? Flick through the museums and galleries in your city. The Venues screen lists alphabetically, while Nearby shows the closest places. Tap a venue to see what's on now. You can also search other cities, or filter for specific venues. Be prepared to wait the very first time you load info for a city—it takes a few minutes to transfer this mother lode of art info. Once loaded, though, the app is peppy and convenient.

MAKE AN ART DATE: The Calendar screen shows events and openings in the area, and you can filter for specific dates or cities. Tap the event to see exhibition details. The app lets you bookmark shows and venues you don't want to miss, and you can also browse by artist names to see upcoming shows or to find out what gallery represents them in your city.

Best App for Finding Live Music

Local Concerts

Free
Version: 1.2
iLike

Tune into Local Concerts' gigantic collection of music listings to find upcoming concerts just about anywhere in the world. The app normally uses your current location to find nearby events and music venues, but you can also ask it to give you results for any other town or city, indispensable for the traveling rocker. The display is simple but effective, showing all the local concerts for the next several days or weeks.

THE FUTURE OF ROCK: The Shows screen displays upcoming concerts in your area. For large cities, that can be way too much music to absorb at once, so the app lets you winnow the list to show only the most popular shows. Tap the All button to browse the big list, or tap Venues to browse what's happening at your city's clubs and music halls.

TICKETS, TICKETS: When you find a show that you can't miss, tap it to get more details, map the venue, or buy tickets. The app is smart enough to know the website of whatever ticket agency or club handles the concert; tapping the Tickets button takes you there to complete the purchase.

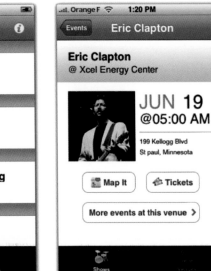

Best Apps at Leisure

 Sure, your iPhone's great for getting stuff done, but let's not kid ourselves. Your glossy gadget is even better for whiling away the hours. For every productivity enhancer in the App Store, there are at least three productivity killers. That's not a bad thing, either: Just like your day-to-day life, your iPhone's app collection deserves a healthy balance between work and leisure. Indulge, and treat yourself to a few fun-loving apps… or more than a few.

This chapter reviews the best apps for kicking back. You'll find **social networking** apps that make it easy to connect with your friends online. You'll discover the best apps for **reading** and **rockin' out.** Feeling creative? Download apps for **making music, taking photos,** and **drawing pictures.** And for moments when you're away from your couch but still crave some quality TV time, you'll find recommendations for **watching the tube** on your phone.

Finally, **just for the heck of it,** you'll dip a toe into the vast category of just plain zany apps. Want to be a James Bond super villain? Wondering where to report an Elvis sighting? Yearning to tend a Japanese Zen garden? Slip ahead a few pages, carefree reader… we've got you covered.

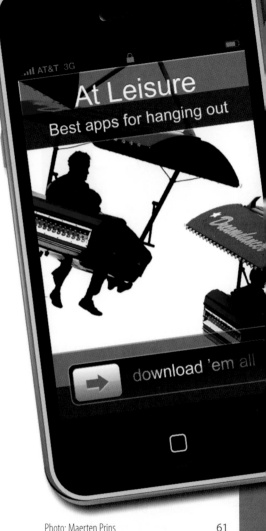

Photo: Maerten Prins

Best App for Facebook

Facebook

Free
Version: 2.5
Facebook

Squeeze your friends into your pocket with the official Facebook app. This compact view of the Facebook universe lets you check your friends' activity, add status updates or wall posts, start a live chat, and share new photos. Sorry, you can't use Facebook's many apps in this mobile version (no quizzes to find out your aura's color or what cartoon character you most resemble), but it's a handy way to keep your profile updated on the go.

HOME BASE: The Home screen shows your news feed, plus notifications and friend requests. Tap the profile button in the top left corner to post a status update. Browse your friends' complete activity by flicking through the full live feed, or zero in on status updates, photos, links, notes, or updates from specific groups. Comments are indicated with speech bubbles; tap to add your own.

GOTTA BE ME: The profile screen puts the focus on your own activity. Scan the wall to see your current status and recent activity. Post a new status update or upload photos to your profile. Tapping the Info or Photos tab brings up your profile details or photo albums.

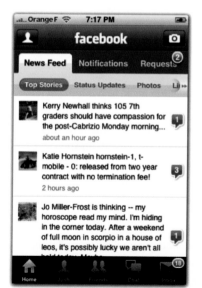

PROFILES A-POPPIN': The Friends screen lists all your Facebook chums. Tap a name to see a friend's profile, including his wall activity and photo albums, or to post a message to his wall. Craving more immediate contact? Tap the Chat icon from any screen to fire up a live chat with any friends currently signed into Facebook.

PHOTO FINISH: Tap the Photos tab from your profile to browse your own photo albums as well as pictures others have taken of you. (You can likewise see friends' photos from their profile screens, too.) Tap a photo to zoom in or add a comment. Upload fresh photos from any profile screen; you can take a new photo or choose one from your photo library.

FriendSync
$1.99
Version: 1.4
Omnigen Solutions

Put a face to a name. This little app grabs your friends' Facebook profile photos and adds them to their entries in Contacts, your iPhone's digital Rolodex. It's a quick and clever way to get photos into your address book.

Armed with snapshots of your friends, your iPhone has visual caller ID, showing the caller's photo when the phone rings. FriendSync can also snap up friends' birthdays, so you'll never forget to send that smiling mug a card. (*Hang in there: The sync can take a while if you've got lots of friends… a good problem to have.*)

Best App for Twitter

Twitterrific
Free (or $3.99 without ads)
Version: 2.0.2
The Iconfactory

There are lots of Twitter apps, many of them great contenders, but this one gets the top pick for its elegant interface, clever filtering, and a flock of chirpy features. Twitterrific captures Twitter's simplicity—great for casual tweetsters—but also makes it easy to sift and act on vast volumes of tweets. Power users will appreciate the ability to filter the timeline, use multiple accounts, do searches, and review hot-topic trends.

FILTER TWEETS: Start off by viewing all the latest tweets from your timeline. Tap the funnel icon at bottom right to limit your view to direct messages, replies, tweets that mention you, or your collection of favorite tweets. Tap a web link to open the page in Twitterrific's built-in browser, where you can twitter, email, or bookmark the page. If you use Instapaper (page 90), Twitterrific lets you save the web page for later reading.

TAKE ACTION: Tap a tweet to select it, then tap the asterisk at the bottom of the timeline to do something with it. If it's just one message in a larger conversation, tap "thread" to see the whole shebang. You can also learn more about the author, copy (or "retweet") the text in a new tweet, or link to the message in a tweet or email. Add greatest-hit tweets to your public list of favorites, or mark them privately to review later.

At Leisure

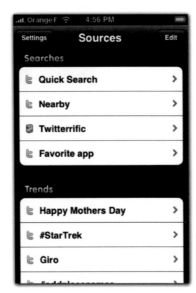

CHIRP AWAY: Post your tweets with a keyboard showing how many of your 140 characters remain. Tap the eyeball below the text area to peek at the timeline of tweets, where you can tap links or account names to add them automatically to your tweet. Icons at the top of the screen squeeze your text (with abbreviations and shortened URLs), upload photos, and update your Twitter profile with your current location.

EXPLORE THE TWITTERSPHERE: Expand your horizons beyond the people you follow. Search all of Twitter for tweets on any topic (the new movie, your favorite book, or your company name, for example), or search for tweets posted nearby. Save your searches to return to them later. Twitterrific also shows you Twitter's current hot-topic trends. Tap one to see the latest tweets for that zeitgeist topic.

What's Twitter?

Twitter lets you share short messages of 140 characters or less with friends, family, and coworkers. It's deceptively simple and addictively engaging. Unlike instant messaging, which invites a reply, a Twitter message (or "tweet") simply answers the question, "What are you doing?" Use Twitter to share what's on your mind, to put a general question to your friends, or to share links to web pages you've explored. Like a message in a bottle, your tweet floats out to the public, drifting to the phones and computers of others who choose to receive them. You likewise tune into the tweets of others—a handful of close friends, perhaps, or hundreds of acquaintances, celebrities, and other twitteristas. It's an effortless way to keep up with your circle. Sign up at *twitter.com*.

Other Apps for Twitter

HONORABLE MENTION

Tweetie
$2.99
Version: 1.3.2
Atebits

Although Twitterrific's spiffier interface and superior approach to filtering tweets give it the edge as best Twitter app, Tweetie is a close runner-up, well worth a look when you're shopping around. It's ideally suited for high-volume Twitter fanatics. If that's you, you'll appreciate a few features that Twitterrific doesn't offer:

Tweetie is especially speedy at loading and displaying tweets, and its ability to fetch older tweets makes it easy to browse as far back as you'd like when you're plowing through Twitter's back catalog. The app also lets you view the followed and following lists of any Twitter author. In addition, Tweetie offers a few interface niceties not found in Twitterrific. A landscape keyboard option gives your fingers some elbow room when composing tweets. And with fewer features overall, Tweetie also feels a bit less cluttered than some of Twitterrific's advanced screens, where you might bog down in the number of available actions.

HONORABLE MENTION

Birdhouse
$3.99
Version: 1.0.1
Sandwich Dynamics

This Twitter notepad is ideal for fussy tweeters who prefer to let posts simmer rather than share them in the heat of the moment. Birdhouse isn't a full Twitter client, but rather a place to park ideas, craft the perfect tweet, store drafts along the way, and even rate them for tweetability. When you're ready, tap Publish to launch your tweet. Change your mind? Tap Unpublish to take it back. Email your draft tweets to back them up or share them offline, which lets Birdhouse double as a nifty general-purpose notepad, too; the ability to export all notes at once via email is a feature lacking in the standard Notes app.

You probably don't need Birdhouse if your typical tweet is, "Eating tuna sandwich" or "Watching rerun of CSI Kansas City." But it's perfect if you have a more writerly approach to Twitter and want time to hone your clever observations. If you take your 140 characters seriously, this app is seriously for you.

Best App for MySpace

MySpace Mobile

Free
Version: 1.4.1
MySpace.com

MySpace mavens get efficient access to profile and friend info with this official app. You can't access music or video—the most popular features of MySpace—but the app nevertheless makes it easy to change your status, view friend updates, add blog posts, and browse and upload photos. And perhaps the best feature of all: The app's clean layout spares you from the, ahem, "creative" site designs of your friends' profile pages.

AT HOME ON MYSPACE: The home screen displays and updates your mood and status. Check friends' activity, or browse and post your own blogs, bulletins, and comments. Other screens from the app's main icon menu let you read and send mail, check friend requests, review friends' profiles, and browse or load photos.

PICTURE THIS: Add photos to your profile by snapping a new picture or choosing from your photo library. Browse photo albums (yours or your friends') by swiping from photo to photo, adding comments or captions along the way.

67

Best App for Instant Messaging

BeejiveIM

$9.99
Version: 2.1.0
Beejive

BeejiveIM is the premium do-it-all instant messenger for iPhone, and it comes at a correspondingly premium price. If either your work or social life revolves around IM, however, you'll almost certainly find the app worth the steep fee. BeejiveIM connects to all the big services and can keep you signed in so you don't miss a message while you're on the run. You can also send and receive pictures, documents, audio, and video.

MASTER SWITCHBOARD: Stay in touch with all your friends no matter what service they use. BeejiveIM lets you stay online with all the major chat networks at the same time. The Accounts screen lets you add and edit accounts, change their status (available, busy, away, or offline), and update individual status messages. Need a new look? Trade in your old chat icon for a fresh photo from your camera or photo library.

SOCIAL BUTTERFLY: It's easy to flit among multiple chats. Double-tap the screen to see the chat list, or tap the top bar to reveal buddy icons for other chats (as shown here); tap a buddy icon to make the jump. Send a photo or voice clip by tapping the camera or microphone icon, or email the chat transcript by tapping the envelope. When you send or receive pictures or documents, you can view the file by tapping its blue arrow icon.

At Leisure

TRANSPARENT CONVERSATION: Tap the chat screen to summon the keyboard, and flip it on its side if you prefer typing in landscape mode. Either way, your typing appears in a transparent bubble, allowing you to see fresh messages as they arrive. Tap the smiley face in the corner to add emoticons to your message.

ALL YOUR FRIENDS IN ONE PLACE: The buddy lists shows your friends from all services and lets you categorize them, edit their profiles, and link them to entries in the Contacts app. You're not limited to this buddy-list gang, though. AIM, GoogleTalk, and Yahoo can send free SMS text messages to phones, too, and Beejive makes this especially easy with a special SMS button on the Chats screen.

Palringo

Free
Version: 1.2.6
Palringo

If 16 bucks is too rich for chit-chat, Palringo is a sturdy (and free) runner-up with nearly all the features, supporting the big IM services along with image and audio messages. It even one-ups BeejiveIM by letting you update your status message automatically with your current location. However, the app lacks BeejiveIM's visual polish and doesn't let you receive and view document files. You also can't organize the buddy list into groups or see buddy icons. But if you can do without those niceties, congrats! You've just saved a few greenbacks.

Best App for Reading Books

Stanza
Free
Version: 1.9
Lexcycle

It was a dark and stormy night... Good thing your book was on a backlit screen. Stanza turns your iPhone into a novel, a reference book, or an entire library. It's packed with features that make it iPhone's most well-rounded book reader, including note-taking, bookmarks, color and font control, and dictionary lookups for squirrelly words. Download a trove of free or paid books, or grab ebooks from your computer with free desktop software.

BRING 'EM ALL: No need to choose among books, Stanza can carry your whole collection. Swipe through your tomes by title, author, or category, or organize them into your own custom lists. Stanza remembers what page you were on when you return to a book, so you can jump right back into the plot.

EASY READER: Controls and menus disappear when you read; it's all about the book. You can read in land-scape or portrait view. Tap the screen's right side for the next page, or left to go back. Hold a word for its definition or to add a note, or tap the top right to turn down the corner and add a bookmark to find the page later.

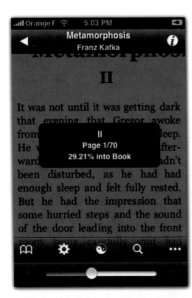

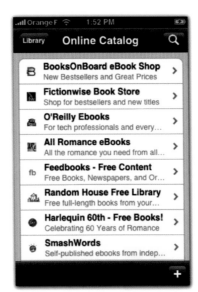

WAY WITH WORDS: Tap the screen's center for Stanza's controls or to return to the library. Use the scroll bar to skim quickly through the pages, or tap the book icon to hop through bookmarks or the table of contents. The gear icon gives way to lots of settings, including font, size, margins, colors, and text alignment. Tap the Yin-Yang to go to white on black, easier for night reading, or tap the magnifying glass to search the book for a word or phrase.

LOAD UP: Download books directly to your iPhone or iPod Touch with Stanza's online catalog. It's actually several separate catalogs, which means you have to browse each one individually. The selection is varied: BooksOnBoard and Fictionwise sell mainstream books; SmashWords offers self-published ebooks; and the Gutenberg Project offers over 25,000 free public-domain books featuring mountains of classic novels.

Books? Really?

Let's be frank: Your beloved iPhone can't compete with old-school wood pulp. You just won't get the same pleasure tapping your way through a novel as you would flipping the paper pages of the real thing. And it doesn't hold up much better against ebook readers like Kindle or Sony Reader, either. The iPhone's battery is relatively feeble, and its screen sports fewer words than a Rambo movie. And yet for all its shortcomings, your iPhone is still the ideal place to stash a book, or even 100, because it's got this one great feature: It's always with you. iPhone books are perfect for filling dead time, for finding relief from the line at the post office or grocery store. Its tiny form makes for easy one-handed reading in crowded subways, and it travels light, carrying an entire library in just a few ounces. It doesn't replace your books; it lets you take them with you wherever you go.

71

Other Apps for Reading Books

 **HONORABLE MENTION**

Kindle for iPhone

Free
Version: 1.1
Amazon.com

No need to buy (or lug around) Amazon's Kindle ebook reader. This app lets you buy and read Amazon's copy-protected digital tomes on your iPhone or iPod Touch; it's the only app with access to Amazon's catalog of nearly 300,000 ebooks. Alas, the reading experience isn't as good as Stanza, with limited customization and clunky, high-contrast text, but the app's easy access to Amazon's vast store earns a nod.

WHAT'S IN STORE: Tap the Get Books button on Kindle's home screen to browse the Kindle store in your phone's Safari browser. Most books offer a free sample, and the purchase process for the full version is fast and easy, as you'd expect from Amazon. The store keeps copies of your books for you and syncs your reading progress; if you happen to be reading the book on other devices, too, Amazon keeps them all on the same page.

TEPID TYPE: Reading in the app is... OK. The contrasty black-on-white text is harder on the eyes than the softer colors of Stanza or Eucalyptus, and adjusting the font size is the only option to change the look. The basics are the same, though: You read in portrait or landscape view, and you flip pages by swiping or by tapping to the left or right. Tap in the center to bring up the settings shown here, where you can add or view bookmarks.

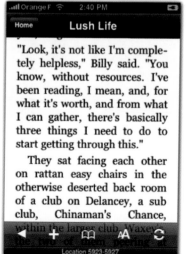

At Leisure

Eucalyptus

$9.99
Version: 1.2
Things Made Out of Other Things

Eucalyptus transforms your ebooks into gorgeous volumes of elegant type and beautifully animated pages, providing the most pleasant, book-like reading experience of any iPhone app. If only it were possible to program the *smell* of a book, this app would nail it. The downside: It can read books only from Project Gutenberg, a free library of 25,000 public-domain volumes, many of them literary classics. But wow, it does it with style and grace.

TURN THE PAGE: The app feels like a classic book, using fancy typography algorithms to create beguiling type quality. Pages curl and fall as you change them. Flick for a quick flip, or drag the page's edge to turn the page slowly. Like Kindle, Eucalyptus offers no customization options beyond changing the font size, but you won't miss it. Every choice from page color to font to line spacing is perfectly gauged for a luxurious read.

CLASSICS: Eucalyptus gathers its books from Project Gutenberg, an expansive collection of books no longer under copyright. Search this library of classic literature by author or title, or get some suggestions from the app's curated selection of picks (shown here). The Eucalyptus staff adds new suggestions every week or two, along with brief descriptions of the works.

Best App for Keeping Reading Lists

Next Read

$0.99
Version: 2.0.1
Square Wheel Software

Remember that incredible book your friend was raving about? The mind-blowing novel that will change your life? Um, no? Next Read helps you keep those must-reads in mind by tracking book suggestions and building or sharing reading lists. It's tuned for recommendations, scoring books based on how you heard about them. Tell the app to favor pointers from literary Aunt Marge but sink tips from lowbrow Cousin Bud.

LITERARY LISTS: Next Read lists the books you want to read, along with Amazon review ratings and numeric scores based on who recommended each one. Tap a book to take notes or browse the Web for more details. Collect books into custom lists (for summer books, work, or fiction, perhaps), or browse by recommender, title, or genre. Email a list, or tap Share to beam it to another iPhone or iPod Touch on the same WiFi network.

SAYS WHO? Next Read ranks books according to how you value the source of the suggestion. The Sources screen lets you add, edit, and assign point values to sources. When you add books, you choose where you heard about it. If the book keeps popping up in conversation, you can add several sources, and the book's position in your list rises to reflect its social capital, buzz, and presumed readability.

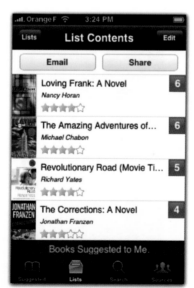

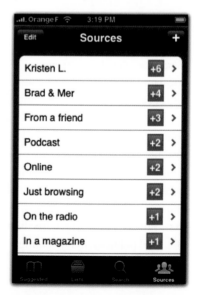

At Leisure

Best App for Finding Indie Bookstores

IndieBound

Free
Version: 1.5
American Booksellers Association

Unchain yourself, and think outside the box store: IndieBound shows you the way to your local independent bookshop. The app's store finder lists the indie stores closest to your current location (or any US address you provide). The app also provides a variety of book lists to find your next read, like chatting with a local bookseller for a recommendation. When you've found a book to buy, the app directs you to the website of a local shop.

LATEST READS: IndieBound's book lists offer picks from the month's crop of new releases, as well as a review of bestsellers and a revolving selection of reading groups. Tap a book to see details, plus reviews from booksellers around the US. Tap the Buy Online button to list local stores whose websites sell the book; IndieBound takes you to the book's page on the site you select, an easy way to support your local bookshop.

LOCAL LITERATURE: Tap the Store Finder icon to see a rundown of the closest indie bookstores. Tap a shop to see its address, phone number, and website. The app also helps you find other independently owned businesses, like coffee shops or movie theaters.

Best App for Literary Trivia

Great First Lines

$2.99
Version: 1.0.3
Moulinarn Mobile Books

It's a game, a book, and a compact exploration of great writing all rolled into one tidy app. Great First Lines collects the first sentence of 200 celebrated novels into flash-card format: Read the sentence and try to identify the book. It's a fun parlor game to play with bookish friends, but it's also a diverting study of language. The lines are arranged in clever order so that each leads thematically into the next, creating a kind of story of its own.

WHAT'S MY LINE? The app is itself an ebook, with a new opening line on each page. Tap the right side of the screen to flip to the next novel, or tap to the left to go back. Tap the Answer button at bottom left to reveal the matching book (here, it's George Orwell's *Animal Farm*).

BOOK BROWSING: Browse opening lines by author or title, a fun reference resource. You can also bookmark favorite lines by tapping the Favorites button below each entry; the app stashes the quote into a bookmark page for future reference.

76

Best App for Dictionary and Thesaurus

Dictionary.com
Free
Version: 1.0.1
Dictionary.com

Give your iPhone a 275,000-word vocabulary. *Dictionary.com* plucks its definitions from the Random House Unabridged Dictionary and gathers 80,000 synonym entries from Roget's 21st Century Thesaurus. The app even coaches you in proper pronunciation with an audio feature that speaks the selected word. The whole thing is stuffed into your iPhone, too—no online lookups—so the response is peppy, no network required.

DEFINITION OF USEFUL: Type your word into the search box, and the app starts suggesting words as you type. Tap the word you want, and the app shows you the definition, pronunciation, word origin and, in many cases, sample sentences. Tap the audio icon to hear the word spoken aloud. Tap Word of the Day to jog your vocabulary with the featured lingo selected by the *Dictionary.com* staff.

TO PUT IT ANOTHER WAY: Tap the dock's Thesaurus button to see synonyms for your word. If you later need to come back for another substitute word, *Dictionary.com* helps you return quickly with its Recent screen, detailing the words you've consulted lately.

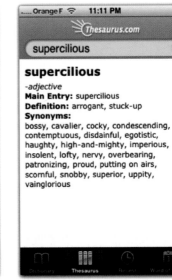

Best App for General News

USA Today

Free
Version: 1.1.1
USA Today

Other news apps offer more depth (New York Times, WSJ) or breadth (AP Mobile), but no other app beats USA Today at quickly scanning what's happening in the world. The app's fast, efficient display lets you hop quickly among sections, articles, sports scores, and daily photo galleries. Participate in one of the newspaper's infographic polls, or share your news discoveries via email, text message, Twitter, or Facebook.

SPEEDY DELIVERY: USA Today does everything a mobile news app should, packing lots of brief, easily scanned items, with any topic an efficient few taps away. In the Headlines screen, swipe through sections at the top, and tap an article to read it, view related photos, or share it with others. You can customize the Top News screen to show the type of news that's most important to you, and of course show the weather for your city.

DAY IN PICTURES: Every day in the app's Pictures screen, USA Today's photo editors show off a gallery of the day's best photos, many of them stunning. Photos are offered in categories, so you can zoom in on sports, space, weather, or—when you need your daily fix of Brangelina—celebrity photos. Flip the picture gallery on its side to see the photos fullscreen in landscape view.

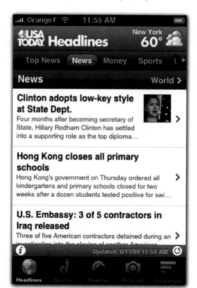

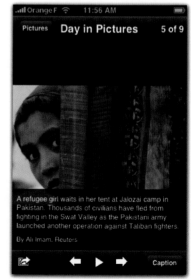

AP Mobile

Free
Version: 3.0
The Associated Press

WSJ

Free
Version: 1.1.2
The Wall Street Journal

AP Mobile gives you access to the whole breadth of Associated Press content, letting you choose from a wide swath of news, photos, and videos from around the world, including your local community. When you first launch AP Mobile, you tell it what corner of the world you're most interested in, and it tailors the news to your location. For US news, enter your zip code, and the app sets aside a whole screen devoted to local headlines. Most folks will prefer to zero in on their home region, but if you prefer, this setup process lets you turn AP Mobile into an app focused entirely on Africa, the Middle East, or Europe, for example.

To manage its huge amount of stories, the app lets you customize the topics to show on the Front Page screen. Even so, the app's display is inefficient, with lots of scrolling, as opposed to USA Today's economy of taps. Still, if breadth and custom-tailored news are what you're after, AP Mobile is the way to go.

It's smart money to have the Wall Street Journal's renowned business coverage on your iPhone or iPod Touch—especially when it's free. The Journal, which normally arrives at your doorstep or web browser for a fee, is completely free in its App Store incarnation. It features an attractive, well considered interface, too, including video and audio reports. The app stores recently downloaded articles on the phone, so you can browse your Journal even when you don't have a network connection (what could be handier for Wall Street's subway commuters?). You can also tell it to save specific articles by tapping a Save button, stowing the page in a list of favorites for later reading.

You browse WSJ's features by tapping section buttons at the bottom of the screen, which you can customize to your whim—moving the paper's iconic What's News icon, off the dock, for example, to make room for a range of other categories.

Best App for Sports Scores and News

Sportacular

Free
Version: 1.4.4
Citizen Sports

The name doesn't lie, this app is honest-to-god sportacular. It's hard to imagine how it could do more to please even the most hardcore news-and-stats sports geek (it even covers rosters for fantasy-league teams). In practice, Sportacular acts like several apps, one for every sport it covers, with the display changing slightly for each one. Choose your sport and then dive deep to wallow in scores, news, team stats, and schedules.

WIDE WORLD OF SPORTACULAR: The app covers all major American sports leagues, including college football and basketball, and European soccer. Tap the icon at top left to switch sports. The Scores screen shows the latest, tap back and forth through dates to see more scores or schedules, or tap a matchup to see the details. Use Sportacular to monitor live scores (it updates every 30 seconds) and get details about games underway.

STELLAR STATS: Sportacular gives detailed stats for every game. Here, the detail page for this NBA finals game shows the starting five players for both teams and summary stats for each. Tap a player to see complete game and season stats, or tap Stats to see all the numbers for all players. Every game has a Comments screen where you and your friends can comment on the game (requires a Facebook account).

HOME TEAM: Follow the news, stats, and schedule for any team; you can also tell Sportacular your favorite teams to follow, and the app makes it easy to pluck out their scores and news. Or build your own team. The Stats option (available from the More screen) lets you build a custom team from players across the league and view their stats, perfect for fans of fantasy baseball, football, and basketball.

MLB.com At Bat

Free lite version / $9.99 full
Version: 1.3.1
MLB.com

At Bat is a solid hit with real-time baseball scores, schedules, and video highlights. But the outta-here home run comes with the full version, with live ballgame audio (and video, too, for some games), a real-time pitch-by-pitch graphic that puts you behind the plate, and live box scores. After the game, the app provides a "compressed game" video with highlights of key plays; you can review play-by-play text descriptions, too. The app expires after the current season, so you'll have to pony up and purchase again for next year.

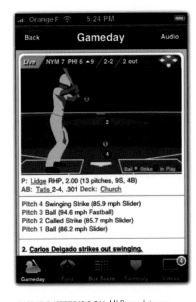

IN THE BATTER'S BOX: MLB.com lets you "watch" any game live thanks to a graphic that puts you in the ump's shoes to see where the pitches fall and how fast. Live audio lets you tune into the play-by-play for every game (the home team's local radio commentary is always available, sometimes the visiting team's, too). Video highlights appear throughout the game for the big plays; tap the Videos icon to watch.

81

Best App for Stock and Market News

Bloomberg

Free
Version: 2.5.0
Bloomberg

If iPhone's simple Stocks app doesn't cut it in your quest to master the markets, give Bloomberg a place on your home screen. The app gives you the whole backstory behind stock and market numbers, letting you drill into major equity indices, for example, to see details about the industry and stock movers. Related news headlines accompany every stock listing, and you can also browse market and business news by any of several categories.

TAKE STOCK: Individual stocks show performance for both the day and the year, along with related news headlines. Flip your iPhone on its side, and the view switches to a full-screen landscape chart: Pinch to zoom in and out on the chart, or flick it backward or forward in time. Go to the Markets screen to track markets around the world, including equities, commodities, bonds, currencies, and equity futures.

MY MARKET: Keep tabs on your personal stock holdings from the My Stocks screen. Enter the stock, number held, and purchase price, and Bloomberg lists the numbers. Tap the column headers to change the display, switching from the current value, for example, to the overall profit and loss of your investments. You can also check other companies from the Stock Finder screen, too, by typing the company's name or ticker symbol.

BUSINESS NEWS: The News screen shows the top headlines for your choice of topics. Tap the Edit button to choose from more than 30 categories to include on the screen, from regional news to industry and market topics to sports and politics. Tap a story to read and, if it's share-worthy, send it along to friends and coworkers via email.

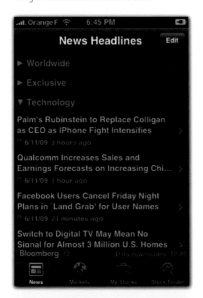

DailyFinance
Free
Version: 1.2
AOL

AOL's DailyFinance is a standout that gives Bloomberg a run for its money. The app outdoes Bloomberg in several places, with gorgeous charts, multiple personal portfolios, and real-time stock quotes (not for major exchanges, though, where there's a 15-minute delay). But DailyFinance doesn't match Bloomberg's facility for checking markets (it doesn't track international markets at all), and its news category layout makes headlines tougher to scan. But hey, why not grab both; at the low, low price of free, they're the right price no matter what the markets do.

REAL-TIME, REAL COOL: DailyFinance is the only free app to offer real-time stock quotes. Tap one of the tabs to see related news and charts. Flip any chart into landscape view to make it sing: Compare performance versus markets or peers, see events like earnings and splits, or compare to any other stock. Tap and hold to summon a crosshair that lets you zoom in on specific data for any point in the chart.

83

Best App for Reading Comics

ComicZeal
$2.99
Version: 2.19
Bitolithic

Zap! Blam! Pow! Bring golden-age comics from the mid 20th century to your iPhone or iPod Touch with this slick comic book reader. The app comes with a small handful of comics and offers access to download more from two online collections, Golden Age Comics and Flashback Universe. Ambitious comic book fans can also scan and load their own comics into the app with the help of free desktop software for Mac or PC.

COMIC COLLECTOR: Browse and download free comics bursting with spacemen, ghoulish tales, and musclebound do-gooders—all with a charming, retro appeal. The app's elegant library collects your downloads into comic bins by series. Tap a bin to open it up and view the individual issues by cover. Partially finished comics are marked with a bookmark, completed ones appear in a plastic bag. Tap the cover to start reading.

PULP ADVENTURES: Read your comics in either portrait or landscape view. Moving around the comic is simple and familiar, like using the Maps app. Pinch or double-tap to zoom in and out, and drag to scroll. Flick a page to the left or right to go to the new page.

At Leisure

Comic Envi

$0.99
Version: 1.1.7
Open Door Networks

Reading the newspaper online is well and good, but something's missing: the funny papers. Comic Envi gives you back your comic strips, presenting the day's cartoons and an archive of previous titles. The app offers standards like Peanuts, Wizard of Id, and Beetle Bailey but also includes online comics like Joy of Tech. There's a wide selection, but the app could be better: It's often slow to load, with several seconds lagging between strips; ads pop up occasionally between comics; and some popular series (like Doonesbury) aren't included. It still makes the cut: For just a buck, you get a daily delivery of comics all in one place.

FUNNIES: The app groups comics by collections, letting you view strips from one series (a Family Circus marathon!) or everything added today. Swipe to the next comic, or tap to bring up the controls shown here. Tap the play button to start a slideshow, or tap the globe to browse the webpage for the strip.

STRIP TEASE: Comic Envi's landscape view typically yields easy-to-read comics, but you can zoom in by pinching the screen for a better look. Drag to move the enlarged image around the screen.

Best App for Browsing Wikipedia

Wikipanion Plus

$4.99
Version: 1.5a
Robert Chin

Wikipedia's big thing is that it's *free*—free to edit, free to use. So why pay for a Wikipedia app when you could just browse online for, um, free? The modest price is worthwhile for serious wikithusiasts: Wikipanion Plus delivers speed and convenience with a browser cleverly adapted to the small screen and the link-heavy encyclopedia. (Yes, yes, an excellent free version of Wikipanion is also available… but without the queue and save features.)

86

SMART SEARCH: As you type in the search box, Wikipanion displays matching Wikipedia articles, letting you type just a few characters to find what you're looking for. In its standard settings, Wikipanion searches only the English-language encyclopedia, but you can tell it to search in other languages, too. Set French as one of the active languages, for example, and voilà, Wikipanion parle français.

PHONE-FRIENDLY: Rather than squeeze original Wikipedia web pages into your small screen, the app uses its own easy-to-read formatting to display articles. Read in portrait or landscape view, and adjust the font size as you like. Tap the dock's list icon to see the article's table of contents, letting you skip straight to the section on gender issues in sumo wrestling, for example. Tap the wavy-lines icon to see related articles.

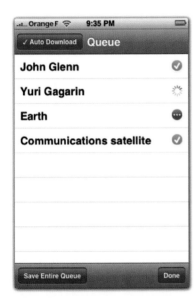

SAVE IT: With so many tantalizing links to related topics, it requires real discipline to read a Wikipedia article to the end. Wikipanion Plus helps by letting you note links to follow later. Turn on the queue feature and, instead of jumping straight to a new article when you tap a link, Wikipanion adds it to a wanna-read list. The app can download articles in the background, so they're ready when you are—useful over slow network connections.

FAVORITES: Tap the book icon in the search bar to see the Bookmarks screen, where you can add, edit, or follow favorite articles. Wikipanion Plus lets you bookmark a specific section of an article, not just the general page (here, the "Venom" section of the Platypus page is bookmarked). Tap the clock icon to see your browsing history, or tap the download icon to see articles you've saved for offline browsing.

PICTURE PERFECT: Tap any photo to see the full-screen version. Tap the photo to download the full-size version and stash it in the photo library of your iPhone or iPod Touch.

Wikipedia apps also make great travel companions. See HearPlanet on page 207.

Best App for Reading Web Feeds

Feeds
$2.99
Version: 1.6
Prime31 Web Design

Web feeds (also known as "RSS feeds" or "news feeds") let you subscribe to your favorite sites, slurping up all the latest headlines in a single app. No need to visit each site to see what's happening; it all comes to one place, and checking the news becomes a lot like checking email. Use Feeds on its own to read and manage subscriptions, or have it sync with Google Reader to let you access your feeds from other computers.

FEED ME: The Feeds app makes it especially easy to find and subscribe to your favorite websites. The Add Feed screen suggests popular newspapers and blogs; just tap an icon to subscribe to a site's web feed. You can also type a website address and the app will subscribe you to the site if it offers a feed (most sites do). If you prefer to go window-shopping for sites, tap the Discover button to search or browse by topic.

SUBSCRIBE NOW: The main screen lists your subscriptions and the number of unread stories in each. Tap a feed to show its articles, or tap Edit to delete, move, rename, or organize feeds into categories. There are also three special categories: Starred Items lists articles you've flagged; All Items combines all feeds into a single list; and Shared Items lists articles you've marked to share with others following your Google Reader account.

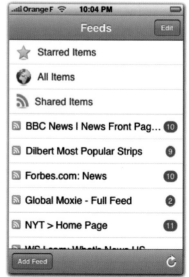

At Leisure

NetNewsWire

Free
Version: 1.0.10
NewsGator Technologies

NetNewsWire offers many of the same features as Feeds, but it's not ideal as a standalone feed reader (you can't use it to add or manage subscriptions), nor does it sync with Google Reader. Instead, it's designed to sync with a *newsgator.com* feed account, which you can access online or by using the popular desktop feed-reading software NetNewsWire (for Mac) or FeedDemon (for Windows). If you use NewsGator or either of those desktop programs to read and manage feeds, then this is the app for you. Otherwise, proceed directly to Feeds.

QUICK SCAN: Each feed lists its latest headlines. Unread items are marked with a blue dot, and read items fade to light gray. Scroll through the list, and tap any items you want to read. When you're done, tap Mark All Read to zero out the the feed's count of unread items. The app updates its feeds every few minutes, but you can tell it to check for new items right away by tapping the Refresh icon at bottom right.

READ ALL ABOUT IT: Many feeds include the full text of every story, and tapping an article shows the whole shebang. Frequently, though, you get only a brief description along with a link to the full page. Feeds has a built-in web browser to handle this so you can read the story without leaving the app, as shown here. From there, tap Feed Actions to share, email, tag, or add the item to Instapaper (see next page) for later reading.

89

Best App for Reading It Later

Instapaper

Free lite version / $4.99 pro
Version: 2.1
Marco Arment

When you don't have time (or attention) to read that loooong article you found online, park it at Instapaper and come back later. It's a simple, free service to store web pages for future reading—no Internet connection required. Instapaper's iPhone app fetches those articles from your account and holds them until you're ready to focus. Even better, it strips out all the graphics, ads, and gobbledygook on the web page, giving you plain text without the distractions.

90

YOU'RE THE EDITOR: The main Instapaper screen presents your handpicked reading list. Here's how it gets there: When you sign up for a free Instapaper account, the service gives you a special bookmark to add to your web browser. When you stumble onto a web page you want to save for later, choose the bookmark, and Instapaper grabs the page. When you next check your iPhone, the page is there waiting for you.

JUST THE TEXT: In its standard settings, the app strips out all ads, pictures, and design from your saved pages, so you can sink into the article text and focus. You can read in either portrait or landscape view. The pro version also lets you: organize and archive articles into category folders; share favorites; browse recommended reading when you run out of your own; and scroll through text by tilting your phone (great for one-handed reading).

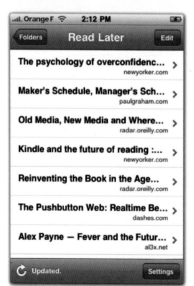

Best App for Naming That Tune

Shazam

Free
Version: 1.7
Shazam Entertainment

Remember that guy from school, the walking music encyclopedia who knew every band and could name every song after just a few bars? Shazam is that guy, only without the attitude. Fire up Shazam on your iPhone (or iPod Touch with a microphone), and the app recognizes, with uncanny accuracy, whatever song is playing in the room, telling you the title, album, and band. It's a great way to settle bets or identify new music.

PLAYING TAG: Shazam refers to its song identifications as "tags." Tag a song by tapping the Tag Now button from any Shazam screen, and the app starts listening to your surroundings. After about five seconds and a quick check with the service's online servers, Shazam tells you what song is playing. The song gets stowed in your personal list of tags for future reference; organize your tags by artist, title, or date.

GOOD LISTENER: Shazam has more than just a sharp ear for music, it knows every band's story, song lyrics, and where to find concert videos. Every song's detail page shows album details, plus song-specific links to the iTunes Store, YouTube videos, and the band's bio and discography. Share the song info via email or Twitter, or add a photo to capture the moment ("Remember Uncle Irving rocking the Black Eyed Peas at the wedding?").

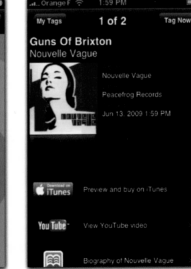

91

Best App for Personalized Radio

Last.fm

Free
Version: 2.1.0
Last.fm

Last.fm is what radio should be: It's free, plays only the music you're in the mood for (no ads), surfaces new music to match your taste, and offers a slew of info about any band when you care to know more. Name a band, and the app plays music from that band and others like it. Tell it a music genre, and it plays music to fit. The more you listen, the more Last.fm knows your likes and dislikes, offering recommendations to match.

RADIO YOUR WAY: Tap "Start a New Station" to play music similar to any artist or category. The "My Library" station plays a mix of songs you've heard in the past; you can build up your playlist by allowing Last.fm to eavesdrop on music you play in iTunes at home or work, so that the app can stream music based on your everyday listening habits. The "Recommended" station plays new (to you) music based on your listening history.

BAND RADIO: Last.fm doesn't play requests for specific songs or albums. Instead, you give Last.fm a band name or music category (a "tag"), and it plays music to fit the genre. The Rolling Stones station, for example, plays music by the Stones but also The Kinks, Hendrix, and The Doors. Tap the heart to love a song, or ban it to tell the app not to play the song again. An "on tour" banner indicates upcoming concerts; tap the banner for dates.

BACKSTAGE PASS: Find out more about the current artist by tapping the "i" button on the song screen. The screen flips to show a detailed bio of the band, with stats of the group's popularity among Last.fm listeners. Tap the dock icons to browse similar artists or see the tags others have used to describe the band. Select a related artist or tag to fire up a new station—a great way to explore undiscovered music.

CONCERT DATES: The Events screen shows a band's upcoming concert dates. Tap an event to see its details, map the venue, or indicate that you plan to attend. When you say you're going to a concert, the app adds the event to your profile, available in the app's Profile screen or at *www.last.fm*. If you give the website your location, the site additionally offers a calendar of area concerts with bands matching your tastes.

Static for iPhone Radio

Internet radio gives instant access to millions of songs (amazing) but also a few headaches (frustrating). Unlike the built-in iPod app, radio apps stop playing when you switch away, and constant network usage drains your battery in a hurry, too. And you might've heard: The recording industry is just a bit touchy about digital music. Stern licensing restrictions straitjacket online services and create awkward limits on listeners. Slacker and Pandora (see next page) limit how often you can skip songs, and none of the services can play more than a few songs per hour by the same artist (a rule that applies to radio stations, too). The rules affect not only *how* you listen to music but *where*: Slacker and Pandora work only in the US (oops, sorry Canada); Last.fm meanwhile plays in over 200 countries, but requires a $3/month subscription outside the US, UK, or Germany.

Other Apps for Personalized Radio

HONORABLE MENTION

Slacker Radio
Free
Version: 1.1
Slacker

Slacker Radio offers free online radio in a gorgeous package, offering band-based stations similar to Last.fm and Pandora, along with a slew of pre-programmed stations in satellite-radio style (Outlaw Country, Alternative Chill, Party Rock, and so on). Slacker also lets you create custom stations, offering more control than other apps in this category by letting you create playlists with specific songs and bands. You create and edit those stations at *slacker.com* and listen to them afterward in the iPhone app.

Listen to Slacker for free, or upgrade to a paid account for $4/month. Paid accounts dodge the commercials that otherwise play after every few songs. The upgrade also buys you song lyrics and lifts limits on song-skipping. (With free accounts, you can't skip songs more than five times per hour; if you hit the limit, you'll either have to suffer through that death metal ballad or start a new station.) *Available only in the US.*

HONORABLE MENTION

Pandora Radio
Free
Version: 2.0.2
Pandora Media

Pandora doesn't offer as many features as Last.fm or Slacker, but keeps things simple with an easy, intuitive interface. You create custom stations by typing the name of an artist, song, or genre as a starting point, and like the other apps, Pandora streams similar tunes. You can also create a new station based on the currently playing song or artist. Pandora is free, but a paid account ($36/year) removes banner ads and lifts the daily song-skipping limit.

Pandora's pretty, too. Flip the app to landscape view, and your playlist history shows up as a series of album covers; swipe to scan the songs you've heard, and tap to see details or buy a song in iTunes. All of the radio apps do a good job at streaming music over cellular networks, but Pandora is the only one to offer an option to help cope with a weak signal, letting you reduce the audio quality in exchange for fewer song drop-outs. *Available only in the US.*

Best App for Traditional Radio

Wunder Radio

$6.99
Version: 1.7
Weather Underground

Spin the radio dial—and keep spinning through thousands of radio stations in every corner of the world. Wunder Radio lets you find radio stations by location or programming format (music, talk, sports); you can even tune into your local weather station or police scanner. Most streams work well over the Edge network, but little icons for each station tell you when WiFi or 3G is required.

TUNE IN: Listen to your pick of thousands of radio stations around the world. Many of 'em provide brief details about the current song or program, and every stream includes suggestions for similar stations to help you discover new broadcasters (bookmark a station to return later). Links take you to the built-in web browser where you can send a Twitter message to the station's DJ, or visit its website.

HONORABLE MENTION

NPR Addict

Free
Version: 1.4
Pass Time Software

While Wunder Radio lets you tune in live to just about any station on the planet, it doesn't help you catch up on the radio you've missed. Public-radio fanatics can do just that with NPR Addict, which offers access to a slew of recent stories broadcast by public radio stations. The big national series are represented here, as well as plenty of local shows. The app's organization is sprawling and at times confusing, but the search feature helps. It's worth digging; there's lots to find.

Best App for Sharing Music

Simplify Music 2

$5.99
Version: 2.1.1
Simplify Media

Take your entire digital music collection with you wherever you go, and tap into friends' music, too. Simplify Music lets you stream tunes across the Internet from your own computer or those of up to 30 friends. It works remarkably well, even over the Edge network, and the whole thing feels like magic. Some assembly required: You have to install Simplify Media's free software for Windows, Mac, or Linux, but it's a snap to set up.

SIMPLE SIMPLIFY: Browsing a shared music collection works like the built-in iPod app. Browse artists, albums, songs, and playlists, and tap a tune to listen. Tap the + icon to add songs to your favorites list, which amounts to an on-the-go playlist. You can access your own computer(s) or those of any friends who have invited you. Because of the small, private scale of Simplify's music sharing, it's all legal and legit.

NOW PLAYING: The current song enjoys an iPod-like display, including album art if it's already part of your home music collection. Tap the Artist tab to see the artist bio from Last.fm, or tap Lyrics to read the words to the song.

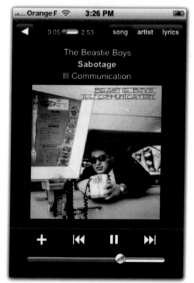

At Leisure

Best App for Remembering Music Tips

NoteWorthy

$0.99
Version: 1.8
Roy Kolak

If you're always stumbling across new music and just as quickly forgetting what it was, let this app be your music memory. Type in the name of the artist you want to remember, and the app fetches the band's albums and tracks, letting you tap any specific albums or songs that have caught your attention. NoteWorthy makes a great pair with Shazam (page 91) to help you remember the bands and music you want to explore later.

BANDS WITH BUZZ: NoteWorthy's main screen shows a rundown of the bands you want to check out. When a friend recommends an artist, tap the + icon to add the band to your list, and the app gives you a search box. Type the name of the band, and NoteWorthy looks 'em up in Last.fm's vast music database, along with the names of all the band's albums and songs.

TRACKING TRACKS: Take note of individual albums or songs from the artist's detail screen. Tap the Albums or Tracks button to browse all of the band's published work, and check off items that interest you. NoteWorthy also grabs the band's bio so you have the whole backstory if you want more info. Tap the list of similar artists to add other bands from the same musical circle.

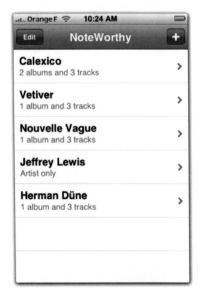

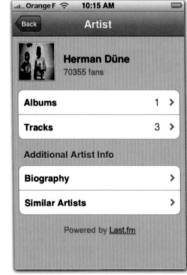

Best App for a One-Man Band

Band
$3.99
Version: 1.4
MooCowMusic

This miniature recording studio lets you layer tracks of virtual instruments to create your own original compositions. If you've got a tin ear, it's fun and accessible, but Band really jams for those with a touch of musical know-how. The app arms you with a piano, a drum kit, a blues guitar, and a bass. Record each instrument as its own track, mix them together, and even sprinkle in some crowd noise for live-performance ambiance.

TICKLE THE IVORIES: Band offers realistic instrument sounds which you mix in individual tracks. Tap the Record button and go. Bang out a drum beat (or use one of the app's eight drum loops), then play the piano, lay a bass line, or riff on the blues guitar. When you've got your tracks, tap Play to hear the whole thing.

GOT THE BLUES: The app's blues guitar makes for entertaining fun even for non-musicians. Lay down the blues rhythm by holding down the left buttons, then come back to strut your lead guitar on the main fretboard. When you've nailed it, save the song to show off your authentic blues to others.

+ HONORABLE MENTION

ZOOZbeat Classic

$2.99
Version: 1.1.7
ZooZ Mobile

This fun little app helps you build a 10-second looping music track which you can share online. Choose your beat (click, hip-hop, pop, or techno) and the app lays down a basic drum loop, to which you add your own mix of instruments. Play by tapping the screen or, much more satisfying, by shaking your phone or tilting it for rhythm effects. The harder you shake, the higher the note. Record a vocal track to add your voice to the mix, then share your musical genius by posting the song online as a MP3 download.

BEAT BOX: The app's hip-hop beat, shown here, gives you separate tracks for scratch, bass, vocal, and synth keyboard sounds, in addition to the snare, bass, and hi-hat drum beats. Your 10-second loop plays constantly; just come in whenever you want, switching instruments to add new tracks, and shaking or tapping to play. When you're done, tap the Menu/Pause button to save or see other options.

Pleasing the Pros

The music-making picks in these pages are fun diversions aimed at mainstream dabblers. If you're a serious musician, don't sing the blues; the App Store has plenty for you, too. The apps listed below are likely to be a bit much for the musical layman, but they're perfect for the toolkit of a hardcore music-maker:

BeatMaker ($19.99) is a pro-level app that combines a drum machine, music sampler, and sequencer into a single remarkable instrument.

Noise.io Pro Synth ($8.99) is a full-featured pocket synthesizer for creating and playing custom sounds on its onscreen keyboard.

iShred: Guitar + Effects ($4.99) is a sophisticated guitar simulator, with options to configure your virtual axe with 2000 chords and scales, plus amp options and pedal effects.

Best App for Performing Live

Leaf Trombone: World Stage
$0.99
Version: 1.10
Smule

Who hasn't dreamt of global adulation for an amazing talent on the leaf trombone? Your moment is now. This app gives you a whimsical instrument and, when you've got the chops, lets you perform live for trombonists around the world. Play songs by blowing into your iPhone and dragging the trombone slider as leaves flutter in to show you which notes to play.

100

SONG BOOK: The app has a giant library of tunes to help get the most out of your leaf trombone. These pre-programmed songs show you where to slide the trombone as you play. After you've got it down, take your act to the world stage and perform it live for three judges listening in on their own iPhones. You're not obliged to perform; you can trombone away on your own, with or without pre-programmed songs.

HONK YOUR HORN: Yes, your instrument is a leaf. With a trombone slider. Hold your iPhone's microphone up to your mouth and blow, using your finger to slide the trombone to the positions marked by leaves flying in from the left. If all this leaves you a little breathless, you can play by tapping instead of blowing (handy for playing on an iPod Touch without a mic).

TROMBONE IDOL: Play songs live for other trombonists, or be a judge yourself. Three randomly selected judges tune in from around the world to listen to the performer, changing emoticon expressions to show how the performance is going over.

JUDGE'S TABLE: Judges rate performances on a 10-point scale, and the score affects the performer's overall ranking. A leaderboard shows the best leaf trombonists in the world, and the curious can review their performances. Judging earns game tokens, which you need in order to perform on the world stage.

Ocarina

$0.99
Version: 1.3.1
Smule

Also made by the creators of Leaf Trombone, Ocarina turns your iPhone into an instrument, this time a musical pipe like a recorder. Blow into the microphone to make a tune, changing pitch by covering the four onscreen holes with your fingers, or tilting to change vibrato. As you play, ocarina broadcasts your tune out into the world. Listen in on others by switching to the app's globe, which spins to show where other ocarinists are playing as their ditties stream your way. A free website lets you manage songs and learn tunes.

Best App for Robot Crooners

Bebot
$1.99
Version: 1.5
Normalware

Let's get the obvious out of the way: Bebot is adorable. Tap or slide your finger around the screen, and your animated robot sings and warbles. Cute! But don't let all this sweetness lull you into dismissing Bebot's ability. Beneath its precious exterior is a sophisticated sound synthesizer with a pile of options to turn your iPhone into a versatile music machine. Bebot delights the kids, sure, but it'll engage musicians and sound enthusiasts, too.

SONG AND DANCE: Tap or drag across the screen to make Bebot sing. Every location on the screen plays a different pitch and volume, and you can use up to four fingers to play multiple sounds at once. You can change Bebot's voice with a wide range of settings; tap the arrow at bottom right to bring up the control panel.

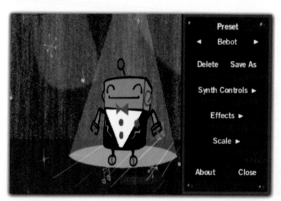

NOT A TOY ROBOT: Use one of several preset voices, or rig your own settings, adding echo or reverb, changing the scale, limiting playback to certain notes, and more. There's some serious sound nerdery under the hood, but mere mortals can figure out the gist with a bit of trial and error (and even the error part is fun).

Best App for Making Meditative Music

Bloom

$3.99
Version: 1.02
Opal Limited

Ambient music pioneer Brian Eno collaborated on this app, and it shows in the app's mellow vibe and arty visual effects. Tap the screen to sound electronic chimes and create corresponding onscreen bubbles. The music loops, bringing the bubbles back, too. Continue to add new notes to the loop, and you create musical and visual layers for a soothing, hypnotic effect. Older loops fade away, replaced by recent notes and new colors.

BUBBLE UP: Every tap of the screen leaves a musical and visual trace, like bubbles or raindrops. The mechanics are simple: Tapping at the bottom of the screen plays a low note, tapping at the top plays high. Your taps repeat in loops as you gradually create a layered composition of sound and color. These echos fade over time, until the screen grows quiet again. If you leave the app idle, it starts to generate its own compositions.

AMBIENT AMBIANCE: Tap the arrow at bottom right to conjure Bloom's settings. Choose a background color theme (each named for a plant or flower), or let the app shuffle them as it plays. The "evolve when idle" option tells Bloom to make its own music and patterns when your own creation is no longer playing.

Best App for Editing Photos

Photogene

$2.99
Version: 2.0
Omer Shoor

Alas, your iPhone's camera is not its strongest point. The fixed lens can't zoom to compose a shot, and colors are often lackluster. Photogene shores up these shortcomings by letting you edit photos on the go. The app amounts to a miniature Photoshop: Crop, straighten, or rotate snapshots, adjust colors and levels, or add text, speech bubbles, and effects. The app saves edited photos to your iPhone camera roll or iPod photo library.

FRESH CROP: Edit photos in landscape or portrait view. Here, the crop tool lets you snip photos to your desired composition. Drag the blue corner handles to highlight the area you want to keep. Tap a button at the bottom to maintain a specific aspect ratio, or tap again to crop freestyle.

STRAIGHTEN UP: Photogene's rotate tool helps you nudge off-kilter photos into place. Drag the slider left or right to rotate the image, and a grid of guidelines materializes to help you stay in line. Tap an icon above the slider to rotate the photo in 90-degree increments or flip it vertically or horizontally.

At Leisure

TALKING PICTURES: The shape tool lets you add speech bubbles to hold text captions. Swipe the shape icons at the bottom of the screen to scroll through your options, then drag a shape into the picture. Double-tap to change the shape's size and position or to edit its text, font, color, and outline. This screen also lets you dispense with the shape entirely, adding text to the photo without a container.

FRAME JOB: Add a decorative border to your photo with one of the many preset frames (swipe the frame icons to see the options), or create your own custom outline in a square, rounded, or oval shape. You can add reflection or vignette effects to frames, or change the background color. The app's filter tool lets you add even more effects, including pencil outlines, heat maps, sepia tone, and green night-vision effects.

COLOR CORRECTION: Photogene offers four tools to edit colors, levels, and exposure. Tap the Levels icon to view a histogram and trim or shift shadows and highlights. If that sounds too fancy, tap the Auto button to let the app handle it for you, adjusting the levels to give colors more pop and sharpness. Tap Exposure to edit brightness and contrast, Colors to edit saturation and temperature, or RGB to tweak the photo's hue.

105

Best App for Atmospheric Photos

CameraBag
$2.99
Version: 1.5.1
Nevercenter

CameraBag simulates old-school lenses and cameras, giving you 10 retro filters to transform your photos and launch them into the past. Take a photo from within the app, or edit a picture from your photo library. Select and preview a camera style to apply, and when you're happy, save the image to your camera roll, or email it to a friend. It's good fun, and the well conceived effects shift the mood of photos dramatically.

PRETTY POLAROIDS: No need to shake it or blow on it. CameraBag's "Instant" filter develops immediately with a spot-on imitation of a 1970s instant photo. Tap the email icon to share your snapshot, or tap the disk icon to save it to your iPhone camera roll or iPod photo library. Tap the filter name to try a different camera style, or grab a new source photo with your camera (iPhone only) or from your library.

SPECIAL EFFECTS: The Helga filter adds a vignette effect, a reference to the Chinese Holga camera of the early 1980s, whose images fade at the edges. Other filters include: the over-saturated "Lolo" filter (referring to Russian LOMO cameras); a fisheye lens; a yellowed "1974" style; the black-and-white "Mono" and "1962" filters; a letterboxed "Cinema" widescreen effect; the "Infrared" filter; and the "Magazine" look for a photo-shoot style.

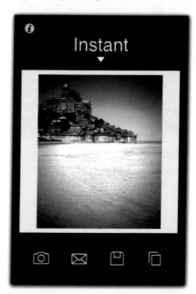

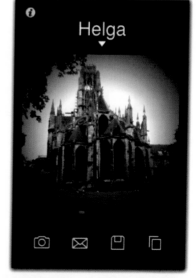

QuadCamera
$1.99
Version: 1.99
Takayuki Fukatsu

Snap a photo with QuadCamera to fill your frame with stop-action images. When you tap your iPhone's shutter button, the app snaps a handful of photos, then stitches the pictures together into a single image saved to your camera roll. True to its name, the app's standard setup gives you a grid of four shots, but you can change the number and arrangement in the app's settings. Switch to a single row of four or eight images, for example, or go with two rows of four. You can also set the time-lapse delay anywhere from 0.1 to 3 seconds.

FANTASTIC FOUR: In addition to capturing time and motion, QuadCamera lets you add photo effects, too. Choose settings to make colors vivid, bright, dull, or high-contrast—or dispense with colors entirely with a grayscale option.

Camera Zoom
$0.99
Version: 1.1
KendiTech

Atmospheric photos are swell, but iPhone's missing zoom lens sometimes means your photos have *too much* atmosphere, your tiny subject swallowed by the backdrop. Camera Zoom helps by providing a digital zoom to let you crop and compose photos as you take them. Use this app instead of the built-in Camera app, dragging Camera Zoom's slider to zoom in up to 400 percent. It's not perfect: The more you zoom, the more you sacrifice image quality. But when you can't get physically close, Camera Zoom provides a good cheat.

Best App for Panoramic Photos

Pano

$2.99
Version: 3.0
Debacle Software

When the wide, wide world presents too much to squeeze into a traditional photo, pour your view into a panoramic image. Pano helps you through the process of building wide-format images to capture vistas, class reunions, or the extremely long line of people waiting to buy the new iPhone. The app fuses up to 16 photos end to end, helping you line up their edges and then blending the seams to make everything tidy. It's easy, and it works.

SWEEPING VIEW: Take your photos from left to right. After each photo, Pano prompts you to take the next, using transparency to show the edge of the previous photo, and help you line up the edges. When you're done, tap the gear-shaped settings button to save the final panorama to your camera roll.

FAR AND WIDE: Pano's results are reliably good, with resolutions up to 6800x800 pixels. The app works best for relatively distant subjects like outdoor views, and it's best to try to limit the amount of detail in the areas where your photo tiles overlap.

Best App for Custom Postcards

Postino

Free
Version: 1.0
AnguriaLab

Having a great time! Wish you were here! Postino lets you share your vacation bliss without ever leaving the beach. The app lets you mail actual paper postcards featuring your own photos anywhere in the world for $2 or less. Choose a photo, type a note, add grandma's address, and you're done; the postcard arrives about a week later. (If paper postcards seem too last century, Postino also sends ecard versions for free.)

PHOTO GREETING: Start off by snapping a photo or choosing one from your photo library. Crop and position the photo as you wish, or add a decorative frame to the photo. After saving your selection, the app prompts you to type a message. There's a sketchpad option, too, which lets you include your signature or even a colorful drawing.

SNAIL MAIL: When you're ready to send it, type the mailing address, or tap the + button to choose an address from your contacts. Mailing a physical card requires a virtual stamp, which you buy by tapping Stamps in the dock. Stamps cost $2 for one-offs, but discounts are available via bulk purchases for as little as $1.60 each. If the price is too rich, send your postcard for free via email by tapping the E-mail tab.

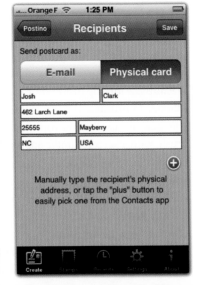

Best App for Sketching or Painting

Brushes

$4.99
Version: 1.1
Steve Sprang

If any app can uncover the painterly masterpiece lurking inside your iPhone, it's Brushes. The app makes your screen a canvas and your finger a brush, with a keep-it-simple approach that's perfect for both quick sketches and ambitious paintings. Its secret is its simplicity: Brushes gives you three realistic brushes, a limitless selection of colors, and that's it. (You provide the index finger.) With so few tools to master, you can focus on your canvas.

SIMPLE OR SUBLIME: While mere mortals will likely make simple sketches, many Brushes artists have made astonishingly complex works. Paint by moving your finger across the screen. Change the brush shape or size by tapping the dock's brush icon, and change color by tapping the eyedropper or color sample at bottom right. The corkscrew buttons let you undo and redo nearly unlimited strokes to clean up unruly paint spatter.

UP CLOSE: Brushes lets you zoom in up to 800% for fine work. Pinch to zoom in or out, and use two fingers to scroll. Paintings are small, the same size as the screen itself (320x480 pixels), and Brushes saves them to your photo library. Mac users, however, can also export to Brushes' free desktop software which can convert images to larger sizes. And get this: The desktop software can even play a movie to recreate your painting stroke by stroke.

At Leisure

COLOR PICKER: Tap the color wheel to choose from millions of colors, using the bars below to adjust brightness or transparency. Transparent colors are great for smoothing transitions, or for tinting the painting with the app's fill tool. As comprehensive as this screen is, it's a lot of work to come back every time you change hues. Instead, daub common colors onto the canvas and grab them with the eyedropper when you need them.

SAVVY SAMPLER: Brushes' elegant eyedropper makes it easy to sample any color already in your painting. Tap the dock's eyedropper button, and a ring circles your finger on the screen, changing color to match what's beneath. You can also get the eyedropper to appear by tapping and holding the screen—easy and convenient.

Sketches
$4.99
Version: 1.6
LateNiteSoft

Brushes is terrific for paintings and drawings, but Sketches is the better choice for casual doodles, notes, and diagrams. The app makes it easy to share your creations via email, Web or Twitter, a social feature that makes lots of sense with the app's emphasis on captioning. Draw on photos (think speech bubbles and mustaches), add notes to a map, annotate a web page, or add an assortment of clip art, shapes, and text to your sketches. It all combines for an app that's at once useful for both jotting notes and exchanging visual gags with pals.

Best App for Font Fanatics

WhatTheFont

Free
Version: 1.0.1
MyFonts

Quick! Name that font! As if you didn't already know, WhatTheFont will tell you that the title of this page is set in Myriad Pro Regular. No kidding: Snap a photo of a typeface, pass it to WhatTheFont, and your iPhone lists the most likely fonts, along with links to buy the typefaces (the app is made by a font retailer). Designers, font fans, and the morbidly curious will find WhatTheFont super-handy. The rest of us can simply marvel.

FONT FINDER: Give WhatTheFont a photo with a typeface to identify, and draw a box around the mystery font, as shown here for "Updike." (What-TheFont works best with a single line of block text; it doesn't cope well with script, for example.) On the next screen, WhatTheFont shows the individual letters that it's found and asks you to confirm that the U is a U and the P is indeed a P. From there, it's ready to find its matches.

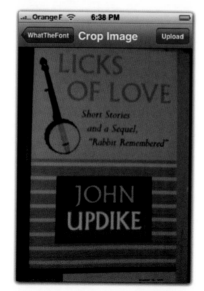

THE TYPEFACE UNMASKED: The app lists the font contenders, showing the most likely matches first. Scroll through the list to find the best match, and tap your selection to get more info. The app provides the link to the font's page at the MyFonts website, which you can either email or visit directly in Safari.

Type Drawing
$1.99
Version: 1.2.1
Hansol Huh

These pictures are worth a thousand words—or at least several letters. Type Drawing is a novel drawing program for scrawling pictures with a stream of type. Type the word or phrase you want to use as your "brush," choose a typeface, and then draw on the screen with your finger. In the standard settings, you get small text when you move your finger slowly and larger type as you go faster. For precise control, you can choose a specific size, changing font and weight for different elements of your drawing. It's a simple concept well executed, and creating these wordplay art installations quickly becomes addictive.

PROPER PUNCTUATION: Symbols and punctuation are useful decorative elements in Type Drawing's doodles. You can change the text and font for your drawing whenever you like, letting you ink different regions in a message or a completely different style.

SKETCHY IDEAS: The app practically demands crafty wordplay. Draw a glass with the words "half full," sketch clouds of nines, or make a ship of "fools." Scrawl your punnery on the backdrop of your choice. The app comes with a pair of grungy paper sheets—white or yellow—as well as blank backgrounds, but you can also use a photo, letting you stencil your type onto any scene.

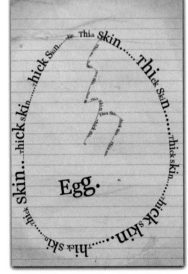

Best App for Planning Your TV Schedule

i.TV

Free
Version: 1.5
i.TV

What's on TV tonight? i.TV has the answer, with TV listings for your area, including cable and satellite services. The app is much more than a TV guide, though: It's a complete personal media planner. i.TV schedules Tivo recordings, manages your Netflix movie queue, screens TV and movie previews, and even offers full episodes of selected series. Want to swap the couch for a movie seat? i.TV tells you what's playing in area theaters.

ON THE AIR: Browse what's showing now. Tap the arrows to jump to the next or previous half hour, or tap the time at top center to choose a specific day and hour. Flip to landscape view for a more traditional grid of listings, showing what's playing over the course of several hours. i.TV lets you filter listings to show only specific channels, program genres, or attributes like high-definition video or closed captioning.

EPISODE DETAILS: Tap a program to reveal its "showcard," with a summary, video clips, viewer ratings, series photos, and links to more info about the series. Tap the thumbs-up button to add the series or the entire channel as a favorite. Tivo subscribers can add the episode to their recording schedules by tapping the Tivo icon or the Watch button, which also lets you set an email reminder or check Netflix for DVDs of previous seasons.

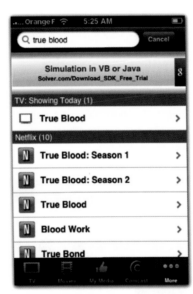

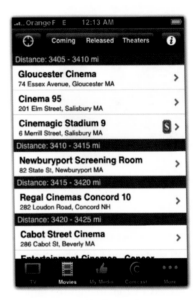

FAVORITES: The My Media screen offers fast access to your preferred shows, channels, movies, and theaters. Tap a favorite show to see series info and a list of upcoming episodes, or tap a channel to see what's coming up. The Now, Day, and All tabs let you set the timeframe, so you can see which of your favorite shows are airing today, for example. Netflix subscribers can manage their movie queues from this screen, too.

A LA CARTE: i.TV's search is especially useful, but you have to hunt for it; the standard settings tuck search on the More screen. Type the name of a TV or movie, and i.TV brings up listings for when it's next showing as well as any Netflix entries for the series or film.

MOVIE LISTINGS: Tap Movies to browse nearby theaters, current films, or coming attractions. Select a theater to see all films playing there; for theaters marked with an icon, you can buy tickets in the app, too. Netflix subscribers who prefer to watch a film after it comes out on DVD can add it to the movie queue from the film's showcard screen.

Best App for Watching TV Shows

TV.com

Free
Version: 1.2
CBS Interactive

Watch clips or, occasionally, full episodes of shows from CBS, Showtime, the CW, and others. The app taps into CBS-owned *TV.com* to offer the same videos found there, but don't get rid of your TV just yet: The app has video from lots of series, but full episodes for only a few, many of them plucked from the archives ("MacGyver," "Star Trek"). Still, it's a good start, with the best TV selection for iPhone outside of iTunes. *Available in the US only.*

TV AT HOME: The home screen shows featured videos. Only a handful of current series, all from CBS, offer full episodes, including "NCIS,""Gossip Girl,""Harper's Island,""Late Night with David Letterman,""Rules of Engagement,""60 Minutes," and others. The substantial library of other programs offer only shorter clips. All programs are available over either WiFi or 3G.

SNIPPED CLIPS: Browse programs from the Shows screen, and tap a series to see its latest videos, almost always a collection of brief clips. For that matter, even full episodes are composed of several "chapter" clips, but *TV.com* handles this reasonably well, automatically moving on to the next chapter of the episode as each clip finishes. Add clips to your personal feed, or mark them as favorites for future reference.

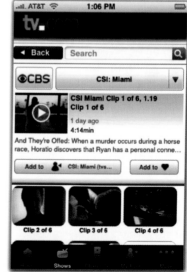

At Leisure

CHANNEL SURFING: Browse programs by channel, or add the entire channel to your custom feed. *TV.com* creates personalized viewing lists based on the specific channels, series, topics, or keywords you provide, as well as your past viewing history. Tap the dock's My Feed button to see what's recommended for you. Or leave it all to chance, and shake your iPhone or iPod Touch to watch a random video.

QUICK SEARCH: *TV.com* offers search results as you type, showing matching series and artists at the top (swipe the black buttons to see more), and specific matching videos appearing below.

Joost
Free
Version: 1.1
Joost

You're bound to find something to watch in Joost's big and bizarre library of full-length TV shows and movies. The WiFi-only service is rich in music videos but has lots of other stuff, too, from nature documentaries to 1970s blaxploitation movies and Hong Kong action flicks. You browse by category (classic films, news programs, sitcoms), but listings are a hodgepodge of latest offerings from around the world (Japanese soap operas!). The result is like grazing a smorgasbord with a blindfold: lots to chew on, but you're not sure what you'll get.

Best App for a Media Remote Control

Rowmote

$0.99
Version: 1.9
Evan Schoenberg

Rowmote provides a simple, easy-to-use remote for controlling audio and video on your Mac or Apple TV. You'll find more sophisticated (and correspondingly complex) remote controls elsewhere in the App Store—see page 30—but Rowmote's appeal is its simple focus on the basic needs of a media player: play/pause, forward/back, and volume controls. If you use a Mac for music, video, or PowerPoint, make this app your remote.

APPLE-INSPIRED: Rowmote borrows the button layout of the Apple remote that ships with some Macs. After you connect to the computer you want to control, use the cross-shaped buttons as you'd expect to start and stop music or video playback. Rowmote connects to other computers on the same WiFi network, with the help of free, easily installed desktop software.

APP SWITCHING: The app commands several multimedia programs on your Mac. Choose or switch programs by tapping the Applications button on the main screen. The remote flips to show the application list shown here. Tap the program to use, and the application launches on your Mac. (This option isn't offered for Apple TV, which has only a single application.)

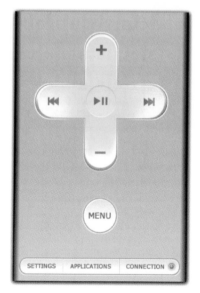

At Leisure

Best App for Mind-Expanding Videos

TED
Free
Version: 1.0
VenueM

Since 1984, the TED conference (short for Technology, Entertainment, Design) has challenged the world's smartest people "to give the talk of their lives" in just 18 minutes. This app streams the audio and video archives of those talks to your iPhone or iPod Touch, letting you listen in on the ideas that excite our culture's leading thinkers in the realms of science, art, government, design, and business. Fascinating and informative.

BIG BRAINS: Sculptors, neurologists, graphic designers, TV producers, world leaders, and bonafide geniuses are just some of the people you'll encounter in these TED talks, which are reliably mind-bending and inspiring.

KNOWN AND NOT: Many speakers are celebrities; others are unknown outside their field. All are passionate about their subject, and you'll be surprised how easily you're persuaded of the urgency of topics you've never considered before—the anatomy of the gecko or the ingredients of dry wall.

Best App for Achieving Zen-Like Calm

Koi Pond

$0.99
Version: 2.3
The Blimp Pilots

Who knew? Turns out a vast number of people harbor the desire to nurture carp. Koi Pond has been an App Store bestseller since the get-go, offering a gorgeous interactive animation of a Japanese water garden. Soothingly hypnotic nature sounds set the mood as colorful koi swim lazily across the screen and under lily pads, nibbling at food you sprinkle on the water's surface. Just like the real thing, that's all there is to it: a relaxing environment.

FISHBOWL: Tap or drag to make the water ripple and the fish scatter. Leave your finger "in" the water, and the fish cautiously approach to take a nibble. Shake your phone to scatter food across the surface, and the fish circle around to feed. After that, all that's left is to watch and enjoy a few moments of koi contemplation.

WATER QUALITY: Tap the bottom right corner to summon the control panel, where you can change the water color, number of fish, and amount of vegetation. Turn the five nature sounds on or off; the thunder sound effect also brings light rain, and water drops dapple your pond's surface.

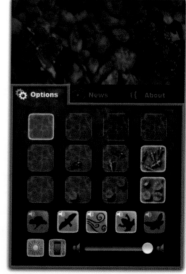

⊕ HONORABLE MENTION

iZen Garden

$2.99
Version: 1.7.3
Random Ideas

For centuries, Buddhist priests have cultivated Zen rock gardens as a ritual of concentration, a study of harmony. And then, suddenly, this ancient art form started popping up in gift shops as cute, miniature diversions for cubicle desktops everywhere. Somehow the effect wasn't quite the same. The iPhone version, however, manages to bring back a hint of the mind-focusing discipline of the original. With meditative chimes and a wide choice of stones and garden elements, iZen Garden turns your screen into a relaxing landscape.

GARDEN VARIETY: Use your finger to rake the sand into intricate and varied patterns. Choose from 100 types of stones, shells, fossils, and plants to place in your garden, or add butterflies to flutter from perch to perch. Make garden elements larger or smaller by pinching the screen, or give them a twist to rotate them. Want to start over? Shake the phone to clear the sand.

PROTECT THE ZENVIRONMENT: The app offers several settings, including a choice of seven background soundtracks like bells, waterfalls, or Tibetan singing bowls. Choose one of four sand colors, select from 100 garden elements, or adjust your rake's size. It's OK to invest some time here; when you leave the app, iZen Garden saves your garden landscape, so it's waiting for you, placidly, when you return.

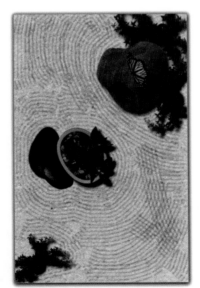

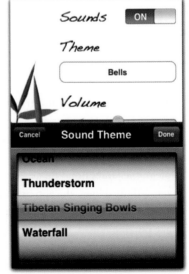

Best App for Bond Villains

Blofeld
$0.99
Version: 1.0
WEsoft

If your scheme to hold the world ransom has been frustrated, or you pine for glory days of Cold War intrigue and toying with Her Majesty's Secret Service, perhaps this app will provide consolation. Named for Ernst Stavro Blofeld, the James Bond nemesis and lover of fluffy felines, the app provides a furry screen, which you stroke to make purring noises. It's the perfect prop for any would-be villain. Diabolical laugh not included.

UNCAGE THE CAT: Double-tap the screen for a choice of feline fur, from Blofeld's classic white to the Mac-inspired snow leopard. The bars open to release your sidekick kitty, ready for your attention.

FIENDISHLY FLUFFY: Blofeld gives you a screenful of your chosen fur. Stroke the screen with your finger, and your iPhone starts to purr. The longer you stroke, the louder it gets (but only when you stroke with the grain; villainous cats are fussy). And that's it: It purrs. Hey, it might not seem like much, but the success of villainous plots hinges on the details, and a proper Bond villain demands a purring cat.

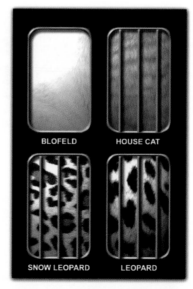

Best App for Aspiring Jedis

Lightsaber Unleashed
Free
Version: 2.1
TheMacBox

In the most satisfying-ever use of the device's motion detector, this app turns your iPhone or iPod Touch into a lightsaber. Brandish your phone in the air, and the app makes the corresponding lightsaber sounds, complete with a dramatic Star Wars soundtrack. Not as clumsy or as random as a blaster, Lightsaber Unleashed is an elegant app for a more civilized age.

ONLY YOU COULD BE SO BOLD: Choosing a character is a fun detail that changes the color and shape of your lightsaber. Tap the "i" icon to see the photo and bio of your selected character. Or build your own: Tap the blue arrow on the Custom icon to add a photo, write a bio, and build your own lightsaber.

THE FORCE IS STRONG WITH THIS ONE: Wave your phone in the air to trigger the app's sounds. Slow motions make the signature lightsaber hum, while faster ones strike spark a clashing sound. It's impressive enough that ridiculous behavior is likely to ensue. Embrace it by mixing in the bold cinematic soundtrack (or send the orchestra home by tapping the music icon).

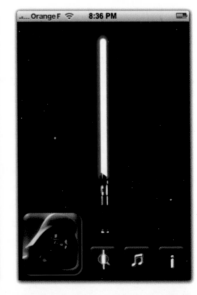

Best App for Emotional Manipulation

Ruben and Lullaby

$2.99
Version: 1.0
Erik Loyer

Ruben and Lullaby are a young couple who, after five months of dating, are having their first fight. That's the setup, and where it goes from there is up to you. The app bills itself as "a story you can play," and it's an artsy if simple exercise in atmosphere. The quarrel unfolds to a jazz soundtrack as you manipulate their moods and expressions. Your actions determine how the quarrel turns out: Do they part ways, or patch things up?

124

TWO SIDES OF THE STORY: The disagreement starts on the park bench, and from there you tilt the phone back and forth to switch your view from Ruben to Lullaby and back again, controlling the reaction of each.

IT'S ALL IN THE EYES: Tap, swipe, and shake your iPhone or iPod Touch to affect the mood of each character. Musical effects accompany your actions, dressing up the soundtrack's jazz rhythm. Try to keep them together, make them split up, or let them keep talking. You pull the strings in this drama.

Best App for Elvis Sightings

Elvis Mobile

Free
Version: 1.0
Resolute Games

Take a little bit of the King with you everywhere you go with this odd little package of Elvis Presley fandom. Browse photos, watch vintage videos, listen to the Graceland podcast, and most crucially: Report Elvis sightings. Alas, the app insists it's not for spotting the man himself, but rather pop-culture references. Still, if you do happen to spot Elvis alive and takin' care of business, your report would no doubt be welcome.

THE VIEW FROM MEMPHIS: The app's webcam shows the current conditions at Graceland. It's a long shot from the estate's gate, but you still feel close enough to smell the fried peanut butter and banana sandwiches. Tap other dock buttons to view a handful of Elvis photos and videos, or tune into the podcast.

SIGHTINGS: Submit your Elvis reports for posting at *Elvis.com*, the official website of the Presley estate. Published sightings include photos of Elvis memorials, tales of meaningful appearances of Elvis tunes, and the inevitable photos of Elvis impersonators.

Best Apps at Play

Even a quick peek at the App Store's numbers reveals that Apple's online emporium is more arcade than office. Games dominate, accounting for three quarters of the most popular paid downloads since the store opened. And it's no wonder: the iPhone is a fun, quirky, and genuinely delightful gaming device. Its limited but intuitive controls—the touch screen and motion detector—make iPhone games accessible to everyone, but fresh enough to grab seasoned gamers. A phone's never been so much fun.

While iPhone can't compare to the gameplay (or battery life) of portable game devices from the likes of Nintendo and Sony, it has a far larger library than its console counterparts, with most titles available for less than five bucks. That means there's no shortage of fun, casual games to enjoy in bites of a few minutes at a time. But with so many choices, it's tough to find the *best* games.

That's where this chapter comes in. You'll start off with action-packed **arcade games** before cooling down with some mind-bending **puzzles.** Settle into a high-stakes seat at the **gambling** tables… or control a person, a city, or the whole galaxy with a **strategy** game. Tackle some **sports,** pick a fight in a **combat** game, then finish on a high note, **taking wing** with a flight simulation. Turn the page: It's game on.

At Play

Best games for iPhone

download 'em all

Photo: Emery Way

Best Arcade Adventure

Rolando

Free demo / $5.99 full version
Version: 1.6
ngmoco

It's up to you to save the cartoon world of Rolandoland and its roly-poly residents. Tilt to roll rolandos through obstacles and avoid menacing shadow creatures. Rolando drips with adorability, from the personable rolandos to the groovy breakbeat soundtrack. Just don't let the high cuteness rating lull you; the game starts gently, but each level (36 in all) presents ever more complex puzzles to test your phone-tilting dexterity.

THAT'S HOW I ROLL: Rolando's controls are easy to master, and the game's a natural for the iPhone's motion detector. Tilt to roll one or more rolandos, and swipe to jump. Many levels require you to escort the kingdom's royalty to safety, pushing the sleeping king or corralling the hyperactive prince.

GIZMOS GALORE: Addressing you as "Finger," rolandos politely ask you to trigger springs, push buttons, spin windmills, or set bombs to help them on their way. Success means getting a minimum of rolandos to the finish, but be careful: Just brushing a shadow creature means curtains for your friends.

Toy Bot Diaries

Free demo / $3.99 full version
Version: 1.6
IUGO Mobile Entertainment

Shepherd a can-do robot through the innards of a vending machine, solving puzzles and navigating obstacles with the help of a grappling hook and a nifty pair of magnet boots. Tilt your phone to navigate the game's four obstacle-packed mazes, restoring your robot's missing memory to finish the game, a feat you'll likely accomplish within several hours. Never fear, though, more diary entries await. The two Toy Bot sequel games (also available for $3.99) each reveal a bit more of the story behind your lovable robot hero.

HOOKED: The robot's grappling hook grabs stuff, letting you drop coins into slots, for example, to unlock doors. Much of the game consists of solving this kind of lock-and-key puzzle, and some of them are real stumpers. Magnetic boots meanwhile let you roam the ceilings or pick up metal objects.

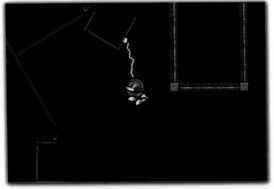

SWINGER: Tilt your iPhone or iPod Touch not only to make the robot walk left or right, but also to swing. Grab hold with the grappling hook and tilt back and forth to get momentum. Before long, you're swinging Tarzan-like from surface to surface.

Best Wacky Save-the-Galaxy Game

i Love Katamari
Free demo / $7.99 full version
Version: 1.0.2
Namco Networks America

The fabulous if spacey King of All Cosmos knocked out the stars in an all-night bender, and it's up to you to gather enough stuff to replace them. The katamari is your instrument: a sticky ball that you roll through living rooms, streets, or entire landscapes, picking up jetsam as you go. Start by rolling up little things, and the katamari snowballs as you go, letting you pick up bigger and bigger objects, like pets, cars, buildings, you name it.

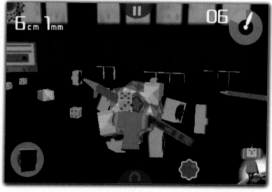

STICKY BALL: Tilt your iPhone or iPod Touch to roll your katamari to a soundtrack of Japanese pop music. Start small, picking up caramels or squid sushi (yes, squid sushi). At first, you bounce off larger objects, but as your katamari grows, you can absorb the big stuff, too.

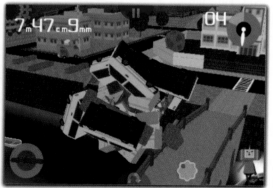

BIG ROLLER: Before long you're rolling up cars and cities. The game offers four types of play: "Story mode" asks you to pick up certain objects; "time attack" challenges you to grow as big as you can in the time limit; "exact size" requires you to roll to a precise diameter; and "eternal mode" lets you roll as you wish.

Otto Matic: Alien Invasion!

$3.99
Version: 1.2
Pangea Software

It's robot versus giant-brain aliens and their radioactive vegetable henchmen! In this fifties-style sci-fi yarn, you control Otto Matic, a heroic robot saving the world from invading aliens. They might have big brains, but you're the one with the rocket boots and ray gun. Save the humans before they're abducted, and travel to alien worlds to rescue captive earthlings. Ten packed levels, a fun retro soundtrack, and a sharp sense of humor make for an engaging, often hilarious adventure.

ROBOT HERO: Steer Otto with the control pad at left and use the action buttons to punch, shoot, fly, or switch weapons. The indicators at the top of the screen monitor your progress. This pile of controls feels a tad busy at first, but once you get the hang of it, the game moves fluidly.

ON THE FARM: The game starts on Earth, where Otto tries to grab humans before UFOs abduct them. Along the way, mutant corn cobs give chase (they pop corn when you shoot them), tomatoes jump you, and sprouts thrash. Escape to your rocket to seek alien planets and take the fight to The Giant Brain.

Best App for Innovative Gameplay

Blue Defense!
Free demo / $1.99 full version
Version: 2.0
John Kooistra

Blue Defense! puts your iPhone's motion detector to novel use with a simple but stylishly challenging game of space invaders: Shoot the aliens before they reach your planet. Hold your iPhone or iPod Touch upright, and tilt to aim. Your bullets always shoot straight up, so as invaders pour in from all directions, you're soon spinning your phone sideways and upside down to keep up with the onslaught. Great, frantic fun.

RED RAIN: The controls are deceptively simple ("That's it? Tilt to aim?"), but the game is wonderfully exacting as hordes of crimson aliens descend to destroy (or, um, impregnate?) your blue planet. The game's retro vector graphics are paired perfectly with a down-tempo electronic soundtrack, which helps keep your pulse low even as the pace of the game quickens. The result is a game that is at once engaging and atmospheric.

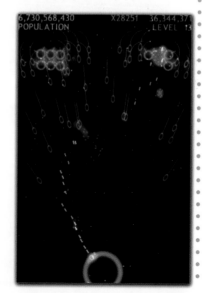

⊕ HONORABLE MENTION

Eliss
$2.99
Version: 1.1
Steph Thirion

Eliss doesn't look like much at first, but beyond its primitive graphics lies a new and abstract multitouch gameplay. Fit colored planets into "squeesars" by dropping solid circles into empty ones of the same color. Pinch planets together or pull them apart to fit. But be careful: The screen fills up fast, and your power drains when different colored planets collide. The chunky visuals, touch controls, and wholesome electronic music combine for a charming, soothing game universe.

Best Tower-Defense Game

Fieldrunners

$2.99
Version: 1.2.3
Subatomic Studios

Tower-defense games are a wildly popular genre that started on the Web and has since stormed handheld devices. You build weaponized obstacle courses to prevent enemies from reaching your "tower," or home base. The App Store has many variations, but Fieldrunners is the best, with cartoony graphics, sound, and music that lighten the mayhem. With three game modes and three difficulty settings, it's a deep game offering weeks of play.

TAKE THE FIELD: Stop your enemies from crossing the battlefield by building a carefully placed maze of weapons. This gauntlet of cartoon artillery includes machine guns, rockets, lightning towers, and, of course, goo blasters.

UPGRADE: You earn money as you defeat enemies, and you can plow that cash back into your defenses. Tap a weapon to upgrade it and make it more powerful, or sell it to remove it from the field. You'll need those upgrades: More and tougher raiders appear with every wave of attack.

133

Best Music Game

Guitar Rock Tour

$4.99
Version: 1.2.0
Gameloft

Fans of Guitar Hero, squeeze into your spandex and prepare to rock your iPhone. Guitar Rock Tour brings the Guitar Hero recipe to the small screen, including 17 familiar guitar anthems (or at least good-quality cover versions). Just like the original uberpopular game, you tap the strings of your guitar in time with colored notes falling toward you, or switch to drums to bang your way through the game's classic and contemporary tracks.

FOCUS ON THE FRETS: The band rocks the background as you play—the game has great animation—but keep your eyes on the bottom of the screen, where you play the strings in time with the falling notes. The audience shows its love while you stay in sync, but they're fickle. Hit a sour note or lose your timing, and the crowd turns against you. When things really go bad, the show's canceled.

CLASSIC TUNES: Guitar Rock Tour offers 17 familiar—and occasionally campy—tunes to play in one of three difficulty levels. Tracks include "Heart Shaped Box" (Nirvana), "Message in a Bottle" (Police), "Smoke on the Water" (Deep Purple), "Walk Idiot Walk" (The Hives), and "Banquet" (Bloc Party). The one false note is a sketchy cover of Michael Jackson's "Beat It!"

Saturday Night Fever: Dance!

$0.99
Version: 1.2.1
Paramount Digital Entertainment

Studio 54, eat your heart out; the best disco in town is now inside your iPhone or iPod Touch. Saturday Night Fever puts you on the dance floor, tapping the screen to the rhythm of four disco classics: "YMCA," "Love Machine," "Shake Your Groove Thing," and "Car Wash." As you play, a dancer grinds and gyrates on your screen with inspired steps and a healthy dose of irony. The game could benefit from more songs, but you do get the original tracks and easily a buck's worth of grins.

DO THE HUSTLE: Your disco alter ego is either Tony (below) or Tyrus, a svelte dance machine with a giant afro. Numbered circles appear with the music; tap them to the beat, following the cue of larger circles that fall into the screen. The game mixes in other steps, too, making you double-tap or drag along a path, and a good streak triggers the sensational disco ball. Challenge friends to a dance-off, either on the same device or over WiFi.

Tap Tap Revenge 2

Free
Version: 2.6.1
Tapulous

Like other music games, Tap Tap Revenge 2 is all about tapping and shaking your phone to the rhythm of the orbs and icons falling at you, but the game adds a few new wrinkles. Not least of these is a big music library; the app comes loaded with a small selection, but lets you download from a library of 150 free songs. Most tracks are no-name bands, but the library does include Coldplay, Nine Inch Nails, Mötley Crüe, and others. You can also step up to head-to-head challenges online, or play against a friend on the same device.

Best Retro Arcade Revival

Galaga REMIX

$5.99
Version: 1.0.1
Namco Networks America

Put on your Kim Carnes cassette, and grab your Charles and Di wedding scrapbook; you're going on a nostalgic arcade trip to 1981. Fans of the early-80s Galaga classic get a twofer in this tidy rerelease. Galaga REMIX includes an exact clone of the original game with its circling bumblebees and tractor-beam thunderbirds, but it also comes with a next-generation update. This "remix" version maintains the fundamental spirit of the original but gives the game a fashion makeover for modern tastes.

NEW LOOK: The remix gives Galaga a facelift with new graphics, weapon power-ups, and boss battles. The right side of the screen shows your progress across a five-screen galactic battlefield. After every fifth screen, you fight a giant boss insect which floods the screen with lasers, bullets and other calamities. This effective update improves on the original while preserving the basics.

IF IT AIN'T BROKE: The game's Galaga Classic version is a pixel-for-pixel, bleep-for-bloop copy of the 1981 game. Both the classic and remix versions offer three options for moving your ship left and right. The best option—and the one used in the app's standard settings—are the simple left and right buttons shown here. You can switch, however, to using a slider or using your phone's motion detector, tilting back and forth to move.

Best Pinball Game

Monster Pinball

$3.99
Version: 1.0
Matmi

You've never played pinball like this before. This charming, eccentric, and altogether inspired game makes inventive use of its virtual environment, morphing into one of six tables as you play. Blast the ball off an edge and into a new layout with its own quirky features. Beyond Monster Pinball's cute visuals and whimsical sound effects, it nails all the basics, too, with realistic physics (tilt!), smooth animation, and great gameplay.

SURE PLAYS A MEAN PINBALL: The game consists of six pinball tables tiled in two rows—three on top, three on bottom. Shoot the ball off the edge to travel to the next table. You lose a ball only when it falls down the gutter of one of the bottom-row tables; on the top row, it simply slips down to the table below. It makes for fast, varied play to keep any pinball wizard on his toes.

HOT BALL: The game's hot-ball feature turns the ball into a glowing orb of plasma, good for double points for the rest of its play. Other tables include features like an electromagnetic vortex which sucks the ball into the center, and an alien-electrocuting mutation chamber. Every table has four flippers, and the game lets you tilt, too: Give your iPhone a shove to change the ball's direction.

Best Action Puzzler

Peggle

$4.99
Version: 1.0
PopCap Games

Cross pachinko with unicorns and rainbows, and you get… Peggle! In this simple but wildly addictive game, you fire a ball into a field of pegs where it ricochets like a pinball, earning points for each peg hit and removing them after each round. The goal is to clear all orange pegs. When you do, Peggle plays a fanfare so over the top, so deliciously triumphant, that even the most jaded gamer will squeal and giggle. No kidding, it's that good.

GOT YOU PEGGED: Take aim with the cannon at the top of the screen and tap Fire to launch a shot. Planning shots pays off, earning "style points" for long shots by ricocheting an orange peg off another across the screen. Hit green pegs for power-ups, and land the ball in the kettle at the bottom for an extra turn.

BIG REWARD: As you hit the last orange peg, the game zooms in and throws itself into slow motion as an orchestra plays a rapturous "Ode to Joy." Now *that's* winning! It's one of many eccentric touches, including the oddball personalities of the ten "mentors" who lead you through 55 levels and 40 challenges.

StoneLoops! of Jurassica

Free demo / $0.99 full version
Version: 1.0
PlayCreek

This prehistoric puzzler combines arcade action with color-matching strategy. Boulders roll along a winding track; you must destroy them before they reach the end. To do that, you launch boulders into the snaking field, adding them to the lineup. Connect three or more of the same color and they blow up. It sounds simple, but it takes strategy and quick thinking to match the right boulders at the right time. The game's offbeat reward system gives "house upgrades" as you clear levels, showing a jungle treehouse getting home improvements. Hey, even cavemen love real estate.

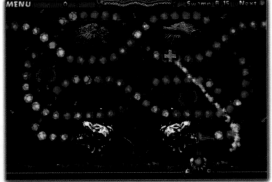

MATCH THREE: You control a cannon at the bottom of the screen that fires boulders into the winding string. When you add the boulder to two or more others of the same color, those boulders disintegrate. The controls are easy: drag the cannon where you want it to shoot, and lift your finger to fire.

POWER-UPS: The game keeps things lively by adding power-ups to the mix, giving your cannon a boost with lightning bolts, meteors, and other effects.

139

Best Tile-Matching Game

LOVE TRIANGLES: The basics are easy, but the game is addictively complex. Group at least three trisms of the same color to make a match. Mind how surrounding pieces will fall in order to plan chain reactions for big scores. Certain combinations create special trisms that fill empty spaces or let you move anywhere on the board. The game throws in troublemakers, too, adding bombs or locked pieces which you have to undo.

THREE MODES: As if the basic gameplay didn't already make for endless possibilities, Trism offers three modes of play. "Infinism" is the standard game, where you play as long as you like in the quest for a high score. "Terminism" is timed play: Earn as many points as you can as quickly as possible. "Syllogism" is a completely different game, where you solve puzzles to assemble tiles just so, sliding them by tilting your phone.

Trism
$2.99
Version: 1.4
Demiforce

Trism is a subtle, mind-bending game of sliding tiles (er, trisms). You play by sliding three or more of the same color together. Move rows up, down, sideways, or diagonally. Matched trisms evaporate, and tiles above fall into the gap, yielding even more matches with a little planning. Here's the fun bit: "Above" is relative. Tilting the phone makes trisms fall in a new direction, so thinking ahead pays off in this brain-busting spatial challenge.

At Play

Best Stacking Game

Topple 2

$2.99
Version: 1.3
ngmoco

Move over Tetris, there's a new kid on the block (on top of another block, on top of another). In Topple, you stack a skyscraper of cartoon shapes as high as you can. Rotate and place shapes for a sturdy tower, but be careful: Put a block down too abruptly or off center, and you'll throw the whole thing off kilter. Your blocks aren't shy about feedback: Stable blocks smile contentedly, but grins give way to anxiety and even panic as the tower wobbles.

BLOCK PARTY: Topple's blocks are vaguely Grinchy, their snide smirks letting you know how you're doing. The fifties cartoon style is matched by peppy period music and fun sound effects, lightening the game's madcap pace. With tough time challenges, you have to move fast but carefully to meet target heights. Shapes rock when you set them down and sway with gravity, but you can tilt your iPhone or iPod Touch to stay balanced.

MORE CHALLENGES: The game moves through six stages, 30 levels in all, and new challenges emerge. Some levels require you to balance two towers on a scale; in others, gravity flips and you have to build your tower from the top of the screen down. As you get the hang of it, you can try to out-Topple your friends in a head-to-head challenge over WiFi or over the Internet via Twitter, Facebook, or email.

Best Word Game

WordJong

Free demo / $2.99 full version
Version: 1.2
Gameblend Studios

Mahjong meets Scrabble in this absorbing, low-key word game. WordJong presents a pile of letter tiles to work into words. The goal is to use every tile, but you can't just take tiles willy-nilly. You may draw only top tiles from the end of a row, and you have to plan ahead to unearth the tiles you'll need later. Earn points for longer words, and try to beat the challenge score set by the game's cartoon WordJong masters.

142

DAILY CHALLENGE: In a quirky twist, WordJong offers only one tile layout per day. Play it as much as you like (every game has lots of possible outcomes), or go back to play any of hundreds of puzzles from previous days. Earn a flower icon by beating the score set by the game's WordJong master for the day.

TILE WORK: Draw tiles to spell words at the bottom of the screen. The game highlights tiles available to draw. Long words buy extra points or bombs that can blow up a tile on the board when you're blocked. Solve the puzzle by using all tiles, and try to beat the master's score or keep playing to improve your own.

Quordy

$2.99
Version: 1.3
Lonely Star Software

Trace as many words as you can in this beat-the-clock word search, perfect for quick, bite-sized diversions. Quordy gives you a jumbled grid of letters, and you identify words by sliding a finger across adjacent letters, including diagonals. The standard game gives you three minutes to find as many words as you can, earning extra points for longer words, but you can also play one-minute, five-minute, or unlimited games. Find out who's got the sharpest eye by challenging a friend to the same puzzle, either online or back-to-back on your iPhone.

EVERY WHICH WAY: Trace as many words as you can. Letters have to be adjacent, but words work in any direction—up, down, sideways, and diagonally. Here, "agate" is traced upward from the bottom of the screen. Earn extra points for words of five letters or more, but be quick. The green timer at lower right counts down your remaining time.

HOW'D I DO? After you finish a game, check how many of the puzzle's words you found. Quordy tells you the maximum possible score and lists every word that was in your puzzle—great for beating yourself over the head. When you challenge a friend to a puzzle, you can do a similar comparison of the words you both found.

Best App for Crossword Puzzles

2 Across
Free demo / $5.99 full version
Version: 1.2.2
Eliza Block

Disciples of the squares, look no further. With 2 Across, you can pluck any of thousands of crossword puzzles from the archives of major papers and work them over on your iPhone or iPod. The app's efficient navigation and flexible puzzle views make it an ideal companion for crossword fans. It's forgiving, too: If you're not sure of an answer, pencil in your letters (instead of using darker "ink") or add multiple letters to a square.

PREP YOUR PUZZLE: Get started by downloading a puzzle from one of the app's many sources, including *The New York Times, The Washington Post, The Philadelphia Inquirer,* and others. Once downloaded, puzzles are stored in the game itself, so you don't need a network connection to work on them. (The app can download the daily *New York Times* puzzles only if you're a subscriber to the paper's premium crossword service.)

GRIDSKIPPING: Swipe the screen to move around the puzzle, or pinch to zoom in or out. Tap a square to select it, and tap again to toggle between down and across. In the "split" view shown here, the bottom panel highlights the clue for the selected square. Tap the pencil to summon the keyboard and type an answer. Not sure? Tap the check-mark icon to see if an answer is correct or to reveal a letter, word, or the entire grid.

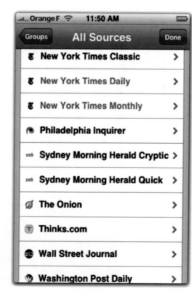

At Play

Best App for Sudoku

Sudoku Unlimited

$0.99
Version: 1.05
Phase2 Media

The App Store is thick with Sudoku games, reflecting the popularity of these number-crunching logic puzzles. Among several strong contenders, Sudoku Unlimited is the best entry, with a functionally limitless supply of randomly generated puzzles, five difficulty levels, and four "skins" for changing the look of your puzzles. The interface is easy and efficient with simple note entry and hints when you're stumped.

81 DIGITS: Soduku can be tough, but its rules are simple. Fill a nine-by-nine grid with digits, making sure no column or row has the same number twice. The grid is subdivided into three-by-three blocks, and these also can't repeat a number. The game starts you with a few prefilled squares, and the rest is up to you. In Sudoku Unlimited, tap a square to select it, and the app highlights its row and column for easy scanning.

SKIN IN THE GAME: The game includes four skins, including this notepad design. All work the same: Tap a square to conjure the number pad. Tap the pencil icon to switch to "notes" mode and jot down tiny numbers to note the square's possible answers. (Here, 4 and 5 are noted as possibilities.) Tap the Auto-Fill icon, and the app does the dirty work for you, filling every empty square with notes of its possible numbers.

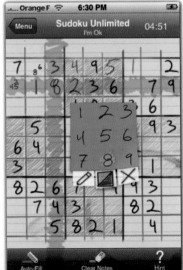

Best Maze Game

Wooden Labyrinth 3D
Free demo / $3.99 full version
Version: 1.3
Elias Pietilä

Tilt your phone to guide a metal ball through a wooden maze, dodging holes and jumping obstacles to a soothing classical-guitar soundtrack. This virtual take on the classic tilting-table labyrinth is beautifully rendered with textures, sounds, and physics so natural that you'll be forgiven if you forget you're holding a phone instead of a handcrafted wooden toy.

146

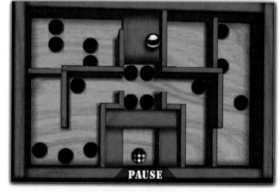

A-MAZE-ING: The game works just as you'd expect, with the ball moving through the maze as you tilt your iPhone or iPod Touch to and fro. But many of the mazes add a new twist by letting you leap obstacles or hop onto platforms. Tapping the screen triggers the jump.

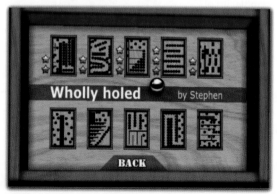

LABYRINTHS: The game comes with 180 hand-designed mazes, organized into series like the one shown here. You can also choose "endless" mode to play an unlimited string of randomly generated mazes, or download user-designed mazes from the app's web-site, where you can design your own mazes, too.

Best 3D Puzzle

Zen Bound

Free demo / $4.99 full version
Version: 1.2.1
Chillingo

This gorgeous, atmospheric puzzle asks you to paint rough-hewn wooden sculptures by wrapping them in string. The string is nailed taut to each figure, and you wrap it by turning the sculpture with your finger. The challenge is to do it with a minimum of string, but really, the appeal is less about challenge than ambiance. Phenomenal graphics and a soothing soundtrack combine for an immersive, remarkable game environment.

BOUND BUNNY: Zen Bound's wooden figures come in all shapes and sizes, from animals to robots, but the object is the same for all of them. Rotate the figure with your finger to bind it evenly with string, as paint spreads out to cover the wood. The game offers three levels of target coverage, and you can stop after the first, or continue along to see how far you can get using as little string as possible.

TREE CLIMBER: The game offers 76 figures to wrap, each arrayed along the branches of a tree in stages. As you climb the tree and complete the levels, paper lanterns light up and give access to the branches above. Tap a figure's wooden tablet to play its level. Even this menu portion of the game is beautiful, the tree swaying with your motions in the lantern light. Amazing.

Best Poker Game

Texas Hold 'Em
$4.99
Version: 1.1
Apple

Sidle up to the table to play the world's most popular poker game against lifelike computer players, complete with twitches and tells, or against your real-life poker buddies over your local WiFi network. Start at the garage location and take your winnings to more luxe tables with higher buy-ins and savvier players. Locations include Istanbul, Vegas, and finally, Dubai. Ante up your five bucks for Texas Hold 'Em: The game pays off in a fun, smart poker game with graphics that go all in.

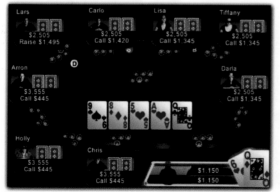

AROUND THE TABLE: Flip the screen on its side for a top-down view, the game's most efficient interface and the best view for putting strategy into play. Follow all players' bets at once, along with their reserves and the pot value. The game offers nearly 150 icons to represent you at the table, including five dogs playing poker, of course.

FACE TO FACE: Eye the virtual players for tells showing the strength of their cards as they bet or fold in each hand's four rounds of betting. Tap players to see where they're from, how old they are, their stats, and a quote (Scarlet: "I won again?! Oh my, it's so nice of y'all to give me all your money"). Your hole cards are tucked in the corner, community cards at center. Bet by tapping your chips, or fold by flicking your cards away.

MotionX Poker

$2.99
Version: 2.0
MotionX

Throw those dice, high roller. This game pits you against the house to assemble the best poker hand from three rolls of five dice. Each die has values for three face cards, an ace, and two sixes which, oddly, represent nine and ten. Hang onto any or all dice between rolls to build your hand; if you roll three aces, for example, hold those to go for five of a kind or a full house in your next two rolls. Shake your iPhone or iPod to throw the dice at a variety of tables you unlock as your winnings grow. It's a simple but addictive game with superb graphics.

ROLL THE DICE: The game pays impressive, mesmerizing, attention to the dice-rolling experience, even changing sounds for new table surfaces. Moving from table to table is one of the main rewards, since there's no big-picture strategy to the game outside of choosing which dice to keep for each hand. Bets are always the same amount, and because they're dice rolls, one hand's "cards" have no relation to the hands that follow.

CHOOSE YOUR WEAPON: MotionX Poker gives you a wide, wide variety of dice to use, adding a new set to your collection every time you roll five of a kind. Many of these sets fit with the game's Orient theme, which plays out in the table designs, music, and sound effects.

Best Game for a God Complex

The Sims 3

$9.99
Version: 1.0.85
Electronic Arts

Take over the life of a "sim," managing his or her dreams, needs, social life, and career in this iPhone version of the popular computer game. Be a jerk by kicking over neighbor's trash cans, become the village Casanova by wooing your neighbors, or brush up on your cooking and gardening skills. Fulfill your sim's whims (buy stuff, slap another sim, get a job, catch a trout) while you keep your charge fed, rested, clean, and uh, toilet-trained.

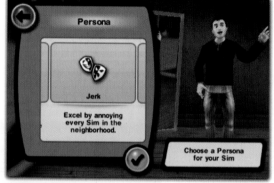

PERSONALITY: Build your sim by choosing its gender, clothes, hairstyle, and most important, its persona. Is your sim a nice guy, a power-monger, a libido-charged sleaze? Your choices determine your sim's personal goals, the actions you can take during the game, and the way other sims respond to you.

GET TO WORK: Much of the game involves tending to the stuff you do in real life: Eating, cooking, bathing, sleeping, working. Take a job at the local lab, town hall, supermarket, or bistro. Your earnings let you expand your house and buy new furniture. Spend your weekends fishing or hanging out with other sims.

HELPLESS: Your sim isn't so bright. It tells you when it has needs, but can't satisfy them without you. Here, a red bathtub icon indicates a hygiene crisis; make your sim hit the shower. You also send it to the toilet, make it food, put it to bed, and entertain it with TV. Take the job seriously: Your sim dies if basic needs aren't met.

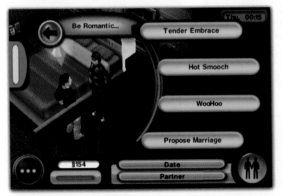

MAKE FRIENDS: Interact with other sims, using small talk, insults, or romantic gestures to develop relationships. Creep out sims by barging into their houses to take a shower, court them with tender embraces, or slap them to make enemies. Brown-nosing pays off, too. Job promotions come faster by bonding with the boss.

Pocket God

$0.99
Version: 1.18
Bolt Creative

If The Sims is about making your sim happy, Pocket God is about making others miserable. You control a tiny desert island of cartoon inhabitants. There's no particular goal or point system; you simply come up with new ways to attack the locals. Flick them into a volcano, feed them to the shark, summon a tidal wave, zap them with lightning, drop meteors on them, attack them with dinosaurs, knock them with coconuts. Let the game's evil cartoon genius inspire you. The game updates regularly, coming up with new forms of spite.

151

Best App for Galactic Domination

Galcon

Free demo / $2.99 full version
Version: 1.5
Galcon.com

Galcon is a nitro-charged version of the board game Risk, launched into space. Take over an enemy's planets by sending waves of ships to overwhelm its forces. The rules are simple—as are the graphics—but the game is endlessly engaging, with ten difficulty settings. Unlike Risk, this fast-paced game delivers cosmic conquest in less than five minutes, ideal for the casual pick-up play that works so well on iPhone and iPod Touch.

GAME OF NUMBERS: Planets are color-coded by player and numbered to show how many ships they hold. Launch an attack by tapping the planets from which you want to send ships, then tap the enemy planet. Here, all the green planets are prepped to attack a single orange planet. When you trigger the attack, ships swarm to their destination and, if your numbers are strong enough, you take it over.

MULTIPLAYER: The game gets more complex as three-front battles develop with multiple enemies. Those enemies can also include human players, thanks to the game's online play, which lets you play against three other players over the Internet. The game offers five other variations, too, including "stealth," where you can't see enemy ships, and "vacuum" where you play timed games.

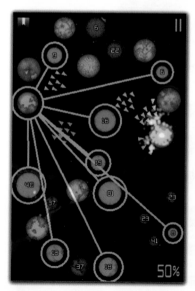

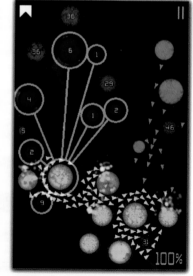

Best App for Urban Domination

SimCity
$4.99
Version: 1.5.0
Electronic Arts

Earn the glory—and headaches—of a city's master planner as you build a thriving metropolis. You're a one-person zoning commission, creating the city's residential, industrial, and commercial areas. Build a power grid, and pave roads to make commerce flow, watching as property values (and tax revenue) soar and dive along with pollution, gridlock, and crime. Your actions decide if your shining city rises or disintegrates into slums.

MUCH TO BE DONE: The game's many buttons show just how much you can do with your miniature city. Build city infrastructure like transportation systems, water towers, police stations, or sports stadiums. Then put on your policy hat to decide whether to raise taxes or change ordinances.

DISASTER STRIKES: SimCity gives you lots of power, but not everything is under your control. Tornadoes, alien attacks, fires, toxic clouds, and earthquakes all conspire to shake your city's foundations.

Best Chess Game

Deep Green Chess
$7.99
Version: 1.1
Cocoa Stuff

Fans of the game of kings will find a worthy opponent in Deep Green, which pits you against a cerebral chess machine or lets you use your screen as a chess board to play a friend. Choose from ten difficulty levels, rewind and watch entire games, or start from any board setup (to match scenarios from chess books, for example). It's pretty, too: The game's elegantly designed board and restrained sound effects offer a pleasant place to play.

THE FIELD: Play unfolds on a love-worn board, where you can play the computer or a friend, or watch the game play itself. Drag a piece to move, and the game highlights the row and column where the piece will land, a nice detail to make sure you're pointing to the right place. You can take back your last move or review your opponent's previous move, or tap the gear icon for a hint when you're not sure what to do.

INSTANT REPLAY: Review a game to watch the action all over again with Deep Green's "playback" mode. Play it straight quickly, step through slowly, or drag the slider to scan for a specific point in the game. Stop the game anywhere along the way, and start playing from there to try a different strategy. A "setup" mode lets you manually lay the pieces, too, to pick up a game started elsewhere or to try a scenario from a book or newspaper.

At Play

Best Checkers Game

American Checkers

$0.99
Version: 1.13
Igor Diakov

Brits call it "draughts," Americans call it "checkers," but you'll just call it fun when you play the game on your iPhone or iPod Touch. This app faithfully reproduces the game on your choice of two boards. Play against a friend, or challenge the computer at any of five difficulty levels to give you an easy win or a brutal spanking. Need to brush up on the rules? The app offers a review and, if you ask for them, hints for your next move.

REFRESHER: The app's help screen offers a quick primer on the basic rules of play. Shown here: the green and white board favored by the American Checkers Federation; you can choose to play on it or opt for a woodgrain checkerboard instead.

WHERE TO? Tap a checker to select it, and the game enlarges the piece, animating its available moves. Here, the selected checker is obliged to jump two white pieces, and a small red checker shows its path upward; tap to make the move. The game enforces the rules of American checkers and lets you move only allowed pieces (if a checker *can* make a jump, for example, it *must* make it, meaning you can't move any other checker).

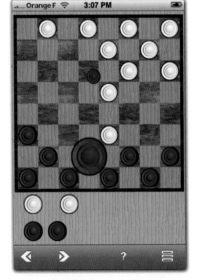

Best Soccer Game

Real Soccer 2009
$2.99
Version: 1.4.5
Gameloft

Goooooaaaaallllll!! This game nails all the details, right down to the familiar goal-time exclamation. Real Soccer 2009 is a vast, impressive game but stays fun and fast with intuitive controls. Any fan of sports video games will get their kicks here, but the game really comes to life for avid soccer fans: 3D versions of actual players from 198 international teams play in 12 stadiums, complete with weather effects, including rain and snow.

LOOK MA, NO HANDS: The basics are easy to master, with a directional controller and two buttons that shoot and pass on offense, or slide-tackle and steal on defense. Flashy combinations of double-taps conjure fancier moves. Your strengths depend on the real-world stats of your chosen team's players.

VARIED PLAY: Real Soccer 2009 offers several modes: penalty kicks, a training mode for practice, five-minute exhibition games, league play, and cup tournaments for longer, more strategic play. It's not just button mashing, either: As coach, you choose player formations, rosters, and substitutions.

Best Basketball Game

Streetball
Free demo / $1.99 full version
Version: 1.0.3
Battery Acid Games

How often do you get the chance to play midnight pickup hoops with the president? Streetball offers three game modes with a choice of cartoon players and, in a nod to Barack Obama's favorite sport, he's one of the options (not speedy, but aggressive and accurate), as is the first lady. The game's cartoonish players are more Pinocchio than Shaq, but the look combines with the game's simple controls for an easygoing, casual sports game.

YOUR BALL: Streetball offers two flavors of two-on-two team play, timed or play to 21. Move by tilting the device, or easier, use an onscreen directional control. Buttons let you shoot or pass, and shooting accuracy depends on pressing the button just long enough to fill an accuracy meter to a target height.

H-O-R-S-E: Streetball also includes a game of horse, where you match shots with the computer until one of you misses five shots the other made. The controls here are quirky if not exactly riveting: The game gives you a squiggly line, and you trace it. The accuracy of the line determines the accuracy of your shot.

Best Golf Game

Let's Golf
$0.99
Version: 1.0.7
Gameloft

Let's Golf hits the links with a pleasantly cartoonish game whose easy-to-use controls make it fun for casual gamers and low-handicap pros alike. Play through four 18-hole courses: You can tee off right away in England or Fiji, but you have to earn the right to play in Scotland or America by playing tournament mode. Or go to "instant play" for a quick game of three holes. Fun play and sensational graphics make Let's Golf a gimme.

DRIVING LESSONS: The game suggests a club, but you can choose another by swiping the icons at left. Tap the map to zoom in on your target and line up your shot. When you're ready to drive, tap the green circle to reveal a meter for power and accuracy, and tap at just the right moment to launch the ball toward the green.

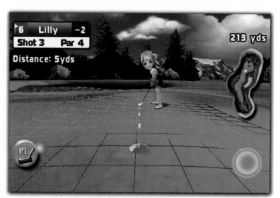

ON THE GREEN: When you putt, the game overlays a grid with pulsing white dots showing the the direction of the green's slope. Adjust your aim appropriately and take your shot.

158

Best Handheld Football Revival

LED Football 2

$0.99
Version: 1.8.1
touchGrove

Kids today! When *we* were kids, we had to *walk* to school… 20 miles through the *snow.* Oh, and handheld video games were giant plastic bricks as big as your head, with tiny screens. *Graphics?!* How about a bunch of blinking red lights, how's that for graphics? Ah, glory days: Rediscover the marvelous Mattel Football with this loving ode to the must-have video game of the Carter administration. Don't forget your 9-volt battery.

RETRO FUN: Run your bright quarterback blip down the field, or pass to your flickering receiver, dodging the defensive LED lights on your way to touch-down. The game offers two difficulty modes, plus two-player action (you pass the console back and forth on turnovers, just like the original).

BANGED UP: The more you play the game, the more the buttons start to show wear and tear, the virtual paint peeling off. Freshen up by flipping the game over (tap the "i" info button on the main screen), and tap the "wear-down" sticker.

159

Best Racing Game

Ferrari GT: Evolution

Free demo / $4.99 full version
Version: 1.2.5
Gameloft

Pack your iPhone with a garageful of no less than 33 Ferraris for this world tour of car racing. Burn through the game's "quick race" mode for fast laps against virtual opponents—or friends over a WiFi connection. Then try "career mode" where you race through challenges to win virtual cash, unlock new courses, and earn access to more cars. It makes a difference: Each of the game's Italian supercars handles differently, playing to varied strengths.

160

RACING THROUGH ROMA: Speed through seven international cities using one of three steering options: tilt the phone, use an onscreen steering wheel, or tap the screen. You can choose to control the gas, or let the game take care of that, leaving you just the brake pedal, as shown here.

DRIFTING: Tap the brake and turn the wheel to "drift," skidding around tight turns. It's a tricky maneuver that takes practice, but you can turn on some car options to help. The game lets you outfit your car with adaptive steering, electronic stability, anti-lock brakes, ceramic brakes, and traction control (handy when it rains).

Crash Bandicoot Nitro Kart 3D

$5.99
Version: 0.7.6
Vivendi Games Mobile

If Ferrari GT packs too much under the hood, give Crash a spin instead. This kart racer dispenses with all the high-falutin' race-car details of more sophisticated racing games, and instead focuses strictly on goofy fun. Tilt your iPhone or iPod Touch like a steering wheel to careen through 12 cartoon race courses. Pick up weapons along the way to bomb, wipe-out, teleport, or rocket past the competition. Pluck fruit from the course, or collect letters to spell out C-R-A-S-H for bonuses along the way. Boppy music and great graphics go along for the ride.

AUTOMATIC TRANS-MISSION: It doesn't take fancy training to drive your kart. No need to worry about brake or gas pedals; the game handles the speed for you, and you just take care of steering. Your car hops to jump obstacles, and you can also press and hold the screen to drift/skid around tough corners.

DRIVE OFFENSIVELY: Race courses are dotted with crates that you can pick up to grab one of eight dastardly weapons. Here, the oil-slick weapon is ready to go. Tap it to wipe out the car immediately behind you.

Best Fantasy Combat Game

Assassin's Creed: Altair's Chronicles
$5.99
Version: 1.1.5
Gameloft

Battle evil from the shadows of medieval cities in this sensational Middle Eastern adventure, featuring rich environments and sword fights aplenty. Altair is bent on avenging a slaughter by the Knights Templar, and you guide him to a chalice which may help end the crusades. The game's much more than hack-n-slash, with mental and physical acrobatics to overcome.

SWORDPLAY: Altair frequently stumbles into fights with Templars, and combat controls are uncomplicated, with two buttons for sword actions (working them together makes some nifty moves). Along the way, you'll also learn to use other gear, too, like grappling hooks and bombs.

KEEP QUIET: It's not all fight, fight, fight. Altair prefers to avoid attention, sticking to the beams and rooftops above the street, and stealth challenges require you to keep a low profile. Even Altair's weapon of choice is silent, a hidden dagger that dispatches enemies quietly without attracting guards.

Hero of Sparta
Free demo / $5.99 free version
Version: 1.0.1
Gameloft

Now *this* game is hack-n-slash. King Argos finds himself the lone shipwreck survivor on an island, and wouldn't you know it, the place just happens to be crawling with every mythical monster in the book—in *every* book, it seems. In order to get home, Argos has to take on minotaurs, demons, the cyclops, some creepy snake creatures, and oh, a side trip down to the underworld. It's all in a day's work for a hero of Sparta. Somehow, all this big-screen action manages to be completely marvelous on the iPhone and iPod Touch, with simple and effective touchscreen controls and impressive 3D graphics.

KING FOR A DAY: Like Assassin's Creed, you move your hero by dragging your thumb across the circle at left, triggering attack and defense actions by pressing the buttons at right. Argus fights with sword, axe, bow, and twin blades, and along the way he finds weapon upgrades, making a tough cat even tougher.

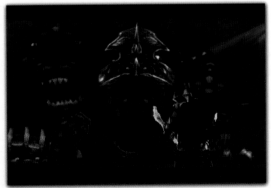

NICE DOGGIE: Three-headed Cerberus gives King Argus a warm welcome at the gates of Hades. The game is full of movies and narrative to add some story between the non-stop battle scenes.

163

Best WWII Combat Game

Brothers in Arms: Hour of Heroes
$5.99
Version: 1.0.3
Gameloft

Accompany the soldiers of the 101st Airborne through 13 missions in Normandy, Ardennes, and North Africa in this 3D shooter. Running through villages of war-torn Europe under heavy Axis fire can make it tough to concentrate on admittedly challenging touchscreen controls, but the game's sound and graphics are, well, dynamite. Worth the effort.

LINE OF FIRE: Fight tanks, soldiers, armored cars, and more in this loud, action-packed adventure. Move your soldier by dragging the joystick-like control at left, aim by touching the screen, and fire with the button at right. Aiming is awkward at first, but it's worth the time (and patience) it takes to get the hang of it.

BEHIND THE WHEEL: Take command of a Sherman tank to liberate an occupied village. As you make your way through the game, you cycle through a whole arsenal of weapons, including Thompson machine guns, bazookas, and grenades.

iBomber

$1.99
Version: 1.0
Cobra Mobile

Patrol the South Pacific as a 1943 bomber pilot tasked to hit a quota of specific targets. Your view of the world is a crosshair, and you tap the Bombs Away button to drop your payload. You have to aim carefully, with enough lead time to account for airspeed, direction, and the type of bomb you're carrying. Turn your phone to steer, and tilt it forward or back to speed up or slow down. Slowing makes it easier to hit targets, but it also makes it easier for anti-aircraft guns to hit you. Take too much fire, and you're going down. The game is colorful and well-crafted with music straight out of a Fifties war flick.

YOUR ORDERS: iBomber offers 12 missions with a set of specific targets to hit. Each mission is set against a new terrain pitting you against new challenges and defenses. Start at Pearl Harbor and go on to target airstrips, island fortresses, and submarines, among other targets.

IN YOUR SIGHTS: Dodge enemy fire as you fly over your target area. The radar helps you find targets, or you can check your list of objectives by flipping on the menu toggle switch. When you've got a target in your crosshair, pound the Bombs Away button to take it out.

Best Flight Simulator

X-Plane 9
$9.99
Version: 9.10
Laminar Research

Categorizing a flight simulator as a game is typically a stretch, since the genre is less an escape than a technical recreation of piloting. X-Plane for iPhone comes from a family of just that type of serious sim, the venerable X-Plane desktop software, but it's been leavened to fit the iPhone. The result is a game that provides a "real enough" experience that's forgiving and fun as you soar over your choice of six beautiful locales.

PICK YOUR RIDE: The app gives you a choice of six small planes to fly. (There are also separate X-Plane apps for fighter jets, airliners, helicopters, and, yes, giant fighting robots.) You can also set the time of day, weather conditions, visibility, and region.

HEADS-UP DISPLAY: The app imposes basic gauge info: Flight speed on the left, altitude on the right, bearing at center. Steer by turning your phone, climb by tilting it back, and descend by tilting it forward. Throttle and flap controls are at the side edges but appear only when you tap there.

HOW'S MY DRIVING?
Step outside the plane to see how you're doing. X-Plane offers three camera angles, including one that lets you zoom and pan around the plane. In this shot, the Beech King-Air is cruising over Hawaii. Other locations include Austria, Alaska, and three California landscapes.

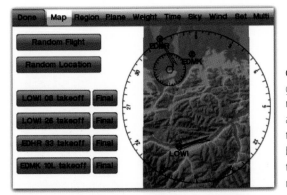

ON THE MAP: X-Plane gives you a map of the region. Pinch to zoom in and out, or rotate the map to match your current bearing. Tap a button to teleport your plane to a new location.

Glyder
Free demo / $1.99 full version
Version: 1.1
Glu Mobile

Unlike X-Plane, Glyder is purely a flight of fancy. This casual flying game gives you a pair of da Vinci-style wings to soar over a fantasy landscape. Nobody shoots at you, there are no monsters, there's no timer in sight. Your only task is a low-key goal to help the game's hero, Eryn, explore six worlds to find hidden gems. Fly by tilting your phone, catching updrafts to go higher. Glyder's worlds make a colorful universe of artfully designed castles, skyways, tunnels, and floating machines to fly around and through for a calm, escapist adventure.

Best Apps at Home

Home is where your iPhone is. That's especially true when you fill it with apps for bringing calm to your castle and discipline to your domicile. This chapter reviews the best apps for managing every aspect of your home life, from your cupboards to your wallet.

Start your tour in the kitchen where your iPhone or iPod Touch gets you **cooking** with tasty recipes and culinary advice. Then it's off to the store with the best apps for **shopping and errands,** helping you manage everything from your grocery list to your car's maintenance schedule—even arming you with consumer info about the stuff on your shopping list. Then again, your iPhone might save you the trip entirely, letting you do errands from the comfort of your Barca-lounger with apps for shopping on Amazon and other online stores.

If all that shopping has you pondering your finances, turn to the best apps for managing your **money and accounts.** Work your stocks, find an ATM, or get an up-to-the-minute view of the status of all your accounts. To better concentrate on your financial empire, impose peace and quiet by calming your brood with the best apps for **distracting the kids.** Or maybe you just need more space: Get home-improvement help or even a brand new home with the best apps for **playing house.** Read on to make your home-sweet-home even sweeter.

Best App for Finding Recipes

Epicurious Recipes & Shopping List

Free
Version: 1.0
CondéNet

Savor 25,000 recipes in a gorgeous wrapper, with online access to *epicurious.com*'s collection from *Bon Appétit, Gourmet,* and other magazines. Heavy advertising may make you wish for a paid, ad-free version, and fans of the website will pine for their recipe boxes. But the app is otherwise delicious and even builds a shopping list for your selected dishes.

HOME COOKING: The Home screen offers six recipe categories for browsing when you need inspiration, or tap "find a recipe" to summon the app's search screen to pinpoint something more specific. The categories are convenient and fit common wants, but it's too bad one of these valuable slots is taken by a redundant category shilling for an advertiser.

CARD CUISINE: Search results and category contents appear as recipe cards labeled with a four-fork reader rating. Swipe to flip through, or tap "view recipe" to see details and reviews. Tap + to save the recipe as a favorite, add it to your shopping list, or email the full text of the recipe. And this is clever: Turn the recipe on its side to display it in big text, with each step on its own screen—no need to squint while you cook.

At Home

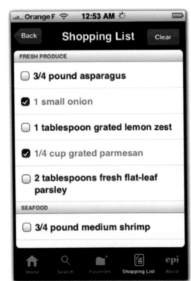

TASTY ICONS: A cookbook is only as good as its index, and the same goes for a recipe app's search form. Epicurious nails this with a clever visual approach for focusing results. Tap a search category (main ingredient, for example) to reveal cute icons. Swipe to browse, then tap one to limit results to, say, duck recipes. You can also leave the icons alone and do a simple search in the search box.

PERSONAL SHOPPER: When you add recipes to the shopping list, the app helpfully organizes their ingredients by grocery department. Tap items to check them off as you make your way through the aisles. It's not perfect—items from different recipes often show up twice—but it's still a handy way to see all at once what you need for tonight's dinner. (See the next page for another shopping-list app.)

Allrecipes.com Dinner Spinner

Free
Version: 1.2.3
All Recipes

Epicurious tends to be more refined, but it's tough to beat *allrecipes.com* for sheer volume, with over 40,000 recipes. The Dinner Spinner app gives you all of them, but with a fun twist to help find a recipe when you're stumped. Like Urbanspoon (page 38), Dinner Spinner offers three wheels to spin or set to find matching suggestions. Choose the type of dish, the ingredient, and the cooking time—or shake to get a random combination—and Dinner Spinner shows you recipes that fit the bill.

Best App for Shopping Green

Locavore

$2.99
Version: 1.01
Buster McLeod

Go figure, but it turns out fruit and veggies taste better when they're not shipped for days on end or catapulted from the other side of the planet. Locavore helps you find local produce and plan menus around food that's in season in your area. The app lists the closest farmers markets, along with opening times and locations. You can also check the current harvest in your area, or figure out just where those February tomatoes are coming from.

TO MARKET: Tap the Markets button to see all the farmers markets in your community (US only). The app relies on the iPhone's GPS to determine your location for this feature. Tap a market to see more information.

WHAT'S FRESH? Tap the States icon to explore what's fresh around the US. The app lists current harvests for every state, with a timer showing how much longer the local growing period lasts. (Here, Virginians should enjoy the year's last taste of local raspberries.) The In Season icon shows the same thing for the state where you're currently located. Tap a food (or choose one from the Food screen) to see a map of where it's currently in season.

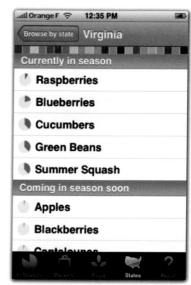

At Home

GoodGuide

Free
Version: 1.2.4
GoodGuide

You've certainly wondered if various products are any good, but have you ever stopped to consider if they're actually... *good*? Good for the environment, good for society, good for the workers who produce them? GoodGuide aims to tell you exactly that. The app taps into the online service at *goodguide.com,* which ranks 70,000 products on a one-to-ten scale based on a range of concerns including consumer safety, health, corporate governance, customer service, and environmental impact. Search for a specific product, or browse categories to find products GoodGuide has judged brimming with goodness.

FOCUS ON THE BEST: GoodGuide offers ratings of four categories of consumer products, and you can drill down into each to browse subcategories and then the products themselves. GoodGuide lists products with the highest rating first, aiming to identify the best products rather than shame the worst. To find the rating of a specific product, tap the Search tab and type the product name to see matching listings.

BEHIND THE RATING: Tap a product to see the details behind its overall rating. GoodGuide assigns a product's overall rating based on scores for three indexes: health, environmental, and social. The summary screen gives only very brief details about the reasoning behind the rating (much more info is available at *goodguide.com*). Food products offer the most detail, with nutritional tidbits and lists of any worrisome ingredients.

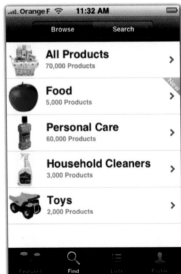

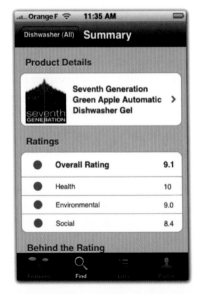

173

Best App for Shopping Lists

Shopper

$0.99
Version: 3.0.2
MidCentury Software

Tuck Shopper into your cart to make trips to the supermarket (or any store) more efficient. Shopper replaces hastily scribbled shopping lists with an organized, uncomplicated system for building and checking off items to buy. The app helpfully groups items by "aisle," or store department, and you can even customize the order of aisles for each store you frequent, so that your grocery list is always organized according to the store layout.

LOTSA LISTS: Shopper can manage plenty of shopping lists for you, useful for juggling multiple projects, stores, or when you simply want to split errands into multiple expeditions. Create template lists to use as starters for future lists (think staples you pick up every week at the grocery store). Tap the + button to start a new list or tap Edit to delete, rearrange, or rename lists. Tap a list to review its contents or start shopping.

AISLE BY AISLE: Each list is organized by store department, or "aisle," making it easy to attack your list efficiently. If you like, you can add specific stores, and choose the aisles each store includes, and in what order (make the dairy department come first at Whole Foods, for example, but don't show dairy at all for Target). Tap the name of the store where you're shopping, and the app filters and reorders the list accordingly.

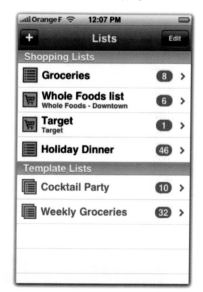

174

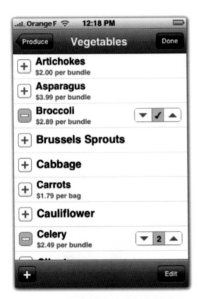

ADDING ITEMS: Shopper's substantial database of products makes it quick to update lists. Tap the + icon from the list screen to search by name, or tap the bin icon to browse items by aisle, as shown here. Scan quickly for what you need, tap items to add to the list, and set quantity by tapping the arrow buttons at right. Add your own custom products, or add and save unit prices to estimate the cost of your shopping adventure.

STORE REMODELING: Choose the aisles to include for each store, and drag them into the order you want them listed when you visit that store. You can add your own custom categories by tapping the + button, which means you can add and organize any type of product you like. You could add aisles for a feed store, a comic book shop, a department store—really, any type of shop you might frequent.

WHEN YOU GET THERE: The app can use the iPhone's GPS to detect when you've arrived at a store. When you turn that option on, Shopper asks if you'd like to switch to that store to see the items you can pick up there. To accomplish this feat of savvy shopping, Shopper lets you set the location when you add or edit a store. Tap the Set Location button to use the current location, or tap the map to choose another address.

Best App for ID'ing That Thing To Buy

Amazon Mobile

Free
Version: 1.1.1
Amazon.com

So you're visiting friends, and by god, but don't they have a handsome toaster. You'd like one just like it, but they don't remember where they got it. You whip out your iPhone, snap a picture, and your phone produces an *Amazon.com* link for the toaster. That amazing magic trick is part of Amazon Mobile, an otherwise workaday app for shopping at Amazon. It does that job just fine, but it's the find-the-product feature that makes it sing.

AMAZON REMEMBERS: Tap the camera icon to photograph a product you'd like to buy, remember, or identify. Within a minute or two, the screen updates with a product name and link, tracked down by an actual human being. Results are great for books, CDs, and DVDs, and good with prints and artwork, too. For toys, appliances, and other stuff, the app often finds an exact match or at least puts you in the ballpark with a lookalike product.

PRODUCT PICKS: Tap the suggested link to see the product details or make the purchase. The toaster shown here is the recommendation based on the photo shown at bottom left. It's not the exact model, but it's certainly the right style. And since two happy customers were excited enough about their toast to give their unit a five-star rating, it looks like a reliable suggestion, too.

176

Best App for Price Comparisons

Save Benjis
$0.99
Version: 1.4.1
Sol Robots

Save Benjis is a coy reference to Benjamin Franklin's mug on the $100 bill, and it does find bargains. Type a barcode number or product name of the object of your desire to fetch prices from hundreds of online stores. It's a quick way to do a sanity check before making a purchase or to find the best bargain when you're shopping online. Using barcode numbers yields the most precise results, although the app can't always identify them.

BARGAINS: Tap a product from the search results to see how its price stacks up at available stores. The lowest price is shown first. Save Benjis has access to 15 million products—certainly enough to keep you and your wallet busy, but not quite enough to cover every item under the sun. Food and clothing have relatively sparse coverage, for example, while electronics and other durable goods are well represented.

WINDOW SHOPPING: Search Benjis hangs onto your search history, making it easy to go back to ogle a product if you need more time to make a decision or later want to refer back to all the retailers selling the item.

Best App for Finding a Bank Machine

ATM Hunter

Free
Version: 1.0
MasterCard

Caught without cash? ATM Hunter shows you the closest place to make a withdrawal. Use your iPhone's GPS to list the bank machines closest to your current location, or enter any address or airport code. Search results let you know the setting for each ATM (gas station, bank, store, and so on). If you're looking for a specific bank or business, you can specify that in your search. The app works anywhere in the world, handy for travelers.

CASH MACHINES: ATM Hunter lists the closest bank machines to your current location or to the address you specify. Tap an entry to see more details about the selected ATM or to map it in the Maps app. To find a specific bank or business, tap the magnifying glass and type the name to find.

ZERO IN: Tap the Filter button on the results page to find specific kinds of bank machines. Find a drive-through, for example, if the idea of parking wears you out.

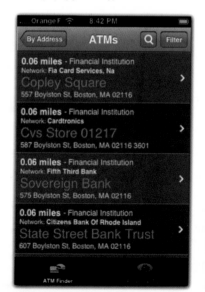

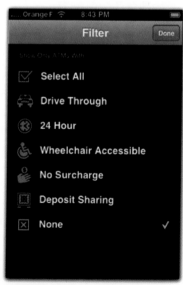

Best App for Car Maintenance

Gas Cubby

Free demo / $9.99 full version
Version: 2.0.1
App Cubby

Gas Cubby garages all of your car's details in a single convenient place to track expenses, maintenance schedule, and gas mileage. Once you've entered a car's info, graph it to keep an eye on overall fuel efficiency, costs, and more. Go full-service by tracking each and every gas-station fill-up, or just enter maintenance checkups to let Gas Cubby remind you when it's time to change the oil, rotate your tires, or even get new windshield wipers.

CAR JOURNAL: Gas Cubby is a diary for your car. Every time you service your ride or feed it gas, add an entry with the details. Track as many cars as you wish; Gas Cubby keeps their records separate for you. Online syncing lets you share entries with another device (so your spouse can update your car's info, too). As you stack up entries, flip Gas Cubby into landscape view to chart fuel efficiency and expenses for your cars.

VITAL STATS: Gas Cubby stores all of your car's basic info for quick reference. Tell it how often you want to schedule service for anything from brake checks to filter changes, or rely on the app's sensible set of standard intervals for these. After the prescribed amount of time or miles have gone by, Gas Cubby alerts you that it's time to take the car in for service.

Best App for Checking Your Finances

Mint.com

Free
Version: 1.0.1
Mint.com

Carry a complete snapshot of your financial picture with this companion to Mint.com, a free online dashboard for monitoring your money. Like the site, the app shows all your balances, activity, and investments at a glance, plus a review of how you're faring against the month's budget. Look but don't touch: *Mint.com* offers lots of info about your fiscal health but doesn't handle payments. It helps you monitor your money, not spend it.

YOUR BALANCE: After you set up a free account at *Mint.com* and give the site read-only access to your accounts, the app's overview screen shows the big picture. Tap to see recent activity or check alerts about low balances or unusual spending. The info comes straight from your bank, credit card companies, and investment accounts, so it reflects only cleared transactions. If the check's still in the mail, it doesn't show up at *Mint.com*.

MONTHLY BUDGET: The *Mint.com* website helps you craft monthly budgets, and the app lets you check how you're doing against your personal spending caps. You can't change the budget levels inside the app itself, but it's a useful way to see if you can really afford that new pair of shoes while you're on the go.

Quicken Online Mobile

Free
Version: 1.2
Intuit

Like the *Mint.com* app, Quicken is a companion to Mint's free rival Quicken Online. The services are similar, but unlike *Mint.com*, you can use Quicken Online to schedule payment reminders and add cash transactions (not just those reported by the bank). That means Quicken knows about upcoming expenses, not just what's in your bank now. The app uses that info to show how much spare cash you've got after the current batch of bills, and a built-in ATM finder lets you get that cash quick.

WHAT'S LEFT: The app devotes much of its main screen to a single number: The cash you've got after expenses. Once you've given the Quicken Online website your schedule of payments, paychecks, and investments, the app tells you what's left for your pocket. Flip your iPhone or iPod on its side to chart your immediate financial future. You can also check recent account activity, log cash transactions, and check your monthly budget.

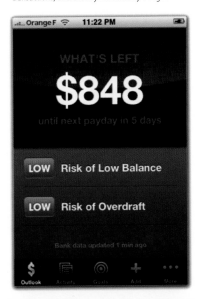

Keep It to Yourself

Mint.com, Quicken Online, and PageOnce (next page) are popular and convenient, and all enjoy solid reputations for privacy and security. But not everyone's comfortable giving financial account info to third-party websites. If that's you, check your bank's offering instead. Bank of America and Citibank, for example, both offer excellent iPhone apps for managing accounts, and most banks at least have websites optimized for mobile devices.

The websites of *Mint.com* and PageOnce both offer options to cut off mobile access if you lose your phone. No matter which service or app you use, however, consider protecting your iPhone or iPod Touch by turning on Passcode Lock in the Settings app. With so much info, financial and otherwise, on the device, you can't be too careful.

Best App for Tracking Every Account

A Personal Assistant

Free lite version / $6.99 premium
Version: 3.5
PageOnce

Okay, so maybe not *every* account… but the gang at PageOnce thought up just about every service you might like to monitor and packed them into a single app, a companion to the free service at *pageonce.com*. See balances and activity for financial accounts, airline miles, cell-phone minutes, Netflix queue, flight times, Facebook messages, and more. The free app is excellent, but the paid version stops ads and includes real-time flight info.

EVERY ACCOUNT IN ONE PLACE: The app's Accounts screen lists all your accounts, packing your whole online presence into a single scrolling view. Tap an account to see balances, recent activity, bill payments, travel itineraries, online purchases, Facebook or LinkedIn alerts, eBay auctions, Blockbuster or Netflix movie activity, and more.

THE LATEST: The Updates screen shows recent changes across all accounts. The Finance screen offers quick summaries of financial accounts and credit limits, and the Travel screen lists all travel-related itineraries (including flight status and delays) in a single chronological view.

At Home

Best App for Online Stock Trading

E-Trade Mobile Pro

Free
Version: 1.2
E-Trade Securities

Customers of online brokerage E-Trade can do their trading on the run with the company's elegant, info-packed app. Review balances and positions, move funds, and place trades. The app also offers expansive market info; after signing into your account, watch real-time streaming stock quotes for any security. (You can use the app for market news even if you're not an E-Trade customer, but you don't get real-time quotes.)

REAL-TIME QUOTES: E-Trade Mobile Pro offers market news and real-time quotes for any stock. Turn on the Streaming option at top right to see a band of red and green blocks flow across the screen indicating moves up and down. Flip the app into landscape view to see an expanded set of info. You can also set up watch lists or browse your portfolio for convenient access to favorite stocks.

BUY AND SELL: Use the app to trade stocks and options (but not mutual funds). For stocks, specify an order type (buy, sell, sell short) and price type (market, limit, stop limit, and so forth), as well as the expiration (good all day, 60 days, fill or kill). The app talks to other financial institutions to let you move money to and from your account.

Best App for Preschool Word Games

I See Ewe

$0.99
Version: 1.4.1
Claireware Software

Introduce your toddler to words for animals, shapes, objects, and colors with two matching games. The first game presents four pictures, and a voice asks your child to tap one of them: "Where is the square?", "Find the zebra," and so on. The game shows the word at the bottom of the screen, too, a good first introduction to sight words. The other game is a classic concentration game, turning over cards to find matching shapes.

184

LISTEN AND LOOK: I See Ewe comes with four sets of "cards" to change the images and concepts in the games. Choose from animals, shapes, colors, and objects. The last includes a miscellaneous collection of teddy bears, balls, TV sets, chairs, and the like. In the app's first game, a woman's voice asks your child to tap one of the cards. An incorrect answer prods, "That's not it," and the right answer gets an enthusiastic "Hooray!"

MATCH GAME: The second game shows a set of six cards, and your child turns them over in sets of two to make matches. Here, too, the audio reinforces the words: "Find another table" or "Look for the clover."

Best App for Preschool Singalongs

Wheels on the Bus

$0.99
Version: 1.0.2
Duck Duck Moose

This inspired children's game combines the interactive elements of a popup storybook with a singalong of the tried-and-true "Wheels on the Bus" song. The app includes several downloadable music tracks to keep the music fresh—and help adults keep their sanity. The app's 12 takes on "Wheels" include versions in German, Italian, kazoo, and, yes, gibberish, but the best is that it lets your kids record their own version to play.

VERSES: Every verse of the song comes with its own interactive illustration. As the music plays, your child can poke and slide objects on screen with satisfying cartoon sound effects (poking the teddy bear makes it hop in the air with a boing).

WIPE AWAY: Slide or tap the screen to make the windshield wipers go swish, swish, swish. Keep on swishing until the end of the verse: raindrops form on the screen if you stop.

Best App for Kids' Jigsaw Puzzles

Shape Builder

Free demo / $0.99 full version
Version: 1.0
Darren Murtha Design

This drag-and-drop puzzle is perfect for kids ages three to six. Drag one of the colorful pieces into position, and it snaps into place. Each of the 100-plus puzzles has a distinct silhouette which, upon completion, reveals itself as an object—a letter, an animal, a fire truck, and so on. Fun, quality sound effects accompany these transformations, along with a voice description of the object or letter: "'U' says 'yoo,' like 'Unicorn'!"

PERFECT FIT: Drag the color pieces into the matching blank areas of the puzzle. Shapes bloop into place with a pleasing sound effect.

TRANSFORMERS: For older kids, part of the fun is guessing what the puzzle will turn into. When the puzzle is complete, its silhouette fills in to reveal a picture.

Best App for Learning ABC's

ABC Animals
$2.99
Version: 1.2.0
Critical Matter

The App Store has a huge number of flash-card games to help kids learn the alphabet, but ABC Animals stands out from the menagerie with its lively cartoon illustrations and a clever device to help kids practice writing letters. Swipe through the cards alphabetically and a voice announces each letter and the pictured animal ("H: Hedgehog."). Double-tap the card for space where your child can trace out the uppercase and lowercase letter.

CRITTERS: Wonderful animal illustrations accompany each letter (thank god for the X-ray fish). Most letters have several animals, and the deck shuffles the new critters into the mix when you launch the app. The game always stacks cards in alphabetical order, and you swipe to flip forward and back.

ANIMAL PRINT: Double-tap a card to flip it over and practice printing the letters. The letters have dance-step-style diagrams showing each stroke and when to draw it. Shake the iPhone or iPod Touch to clear the slate and start again.

Best App for Hidden Object Games

Everest: Hidden Expedition
Free demo / $1.99 full version
Version: 1.1
Big Fish Games

188

This picture-in-a-picture game challenges kids (and you, too) to find objects hidden inside lush illustrations and photos. Well camouflaged objects make for tough work, but the app doles out hints when you're stumped. The game cleverly deploys its dozens of puzzles in a story that follows a reality-show race to the top of Everest. It's an absorbing game for everyone.

THE RACE IS ON: You compete for time against the computer's three teams in a tongue-in-cheek swipe at reality shows like The Amazing Race. As you work to solve the puzzles, the progress of each team is shown in a meter at the bottom of the screen, a novel way to add some low-key time pressure to each puzzle. Take as long as you want, or do your best to beat the other teams.

GORGEOUS PUZZLES: The game's beautifully rendered illustrations and photos give its puzzles rich atmosphere. Pinch to zoom and swipe to scroll as you hunt for the laundry list of items assigned at screen bottom. Tap objects as you find them, but take care to tap the right one; you lose ground against other teams when you grab objects not in your list. The Hint button helps find stubborn objects, but you can use it only every few minutes.

Best App for a Virtual Doll

iChalky

$0.99
Version: 1.2
Eric Metois

Give your kid a little friend to play with—or more likely, to torment. The app gives you a stick figure, Chalky, who walks, moves, dances, and tumbles as you tilt and move your iPhone. Chalky's all jangly limbs, seemingly made of rubber bands. Stretch him, toss him, tilt him, and he comes back for more, walking and stumbling to regain his balance. Your kids will enjoy abusing this little guy, but hey, it's better than torturing the cat.

TINY DANCER: Chalky moves and walks around the screen as you turn the phone, struggling to stay upright. Tilt the phone forward or rotate it all the way around to send Chalky to the ceiling. The little guy can dance, too, moving to the rhythm of music or sound from your iPhone's microphone.

STICK-FIGURE HAZING: Grab Chalky by his head, hands, or feet to drag or throw him around the screen (his expression changes to show his dismay). Keep him dangling by tapping the pushpin icon at bottom left, which pins him in place until you tap it again. Other tricks include replacing Chalky's head with a face from your photo collection, a fine way to work out frustrations on anyone in your photo library.

Best App for Stealth History Lessons

The Oregon Trail

$4.99
Version: 1.1.8
Gameloft

Westward, ho! This terrific remake of the venerable 1970s edutainment title will absorb your child or tween so completely that they'll never see the learning coming. Guide a pioneer family west on the perilous Oregon Trail. Hunt for food, ford rivers, side-step dubious characters, and dodge dysentery. History lessons dot the trail without distracting from the game, giving an effective sense of the hard realities for 19th-century pioneers.

GOOD EATIN': Keep your familily and oxen fed and healthy by foraging for food (like buffalo roadkill, shown here) and by hunting, fishing, or berry-picking as part of the game's eight skill-based mini-games. Meters at the top of the screen show your health, food supply, cash, and miles to go until the next stop.

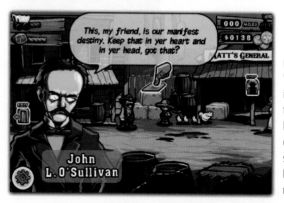

BITE-SIZED HISTORY: "Quest" side missions introduce you to historical figures (like journalist John L. O'Sullivan who championed the westward expansion). Samuel Morse, Abe Lincoln, and many others make cameos, too.

Best App for Young Entrepreneurs

Lemonade Stand

$0.99
Version: 1.6
Maverick Software

Like The Oregon Trail, Lemonade Stand is another update of a classic computer game, this one offering a lesson in sidewalk capitalism. From (lemon) seed capital of $2, you build a lemonade empire, using weather forecasts and headlines to gauge daily demand, adjust recipes, set prices, and make signs. The game's homage to the 1970s version is perhaps too loyal, using the original bleep-bloop music and sound effects, but it remains tasty.

MARKET RESEARCH: Build each day's business plan around the morning headline. Hot weather means more people, and you'll improve sales by adding more ice to your recipe. When there's a convention in town, you can get away with charging more, since the game's visiting businessmen are less price sensitive. (They also prefer their lemonade sour, the game informs you.)

BALANCE SHEET: After you choose the amount, cost, recipe, and ad budget for the day's lemonade, the game shows you the resulting sales, adjusting your bottom line accordingly. You can play "career mode" which lets you keep on going to pursue the highest score, or "classic mode" which lasts 30 rounds.

Lemonville Times
Weather: Sunny
Holiday parade today, huge crowds expected!

LemonCo.

Financial Report, Day 5	
Glasses sold	39
Price per glass	$0.20
Income	$7.80
Glasses made	39
Cost per glass	$0.06
Lemonade Cost	$2.34
Signs made	3
Cost per sign	$0.15
Ad Cost	$0.45
Profit	$5.01
Assets	**$7.81**

Best App for Home Improvements

iHandy Carpenter

$1.99
Version: 1.7
iHandySoft

Put five measuring and balance tools in your iPhone's toolkit. iHandy Carpenter includes a plumb bob (pictured in the icon above), surface level, bubble level bar, protractor, and ruler. Not only are these tools functional, they're also gorgeous, with woodgrain and lighting effects that make them seem straight out of Leonardo da Vinci's workshop. The plumb bob and levels can (and should) be calibrated to make sure you get level results.

ON THE LEVEL: The surface level uses a traditional bubble to show if the iPhone is level but also displays precise angular measures when you want to measure the slope of a surface. Tap the crosshair button to calibrate the balance, setting its current position to zero.

PROTRACTOR: Measure angles, both clockwise and counter-clockwise, with the protractor. Tap anywhere on the screen to set the angle through that spot.

Carpenter's Helper Pro

Free demo / $9.99 full version
Version: 1.0
My Pie Interactive

This advanced construction calculator handles all the math so you can get down to building. Special function buttons make it easy to calculate circle areas, column volumes, and the pitch, rise, run, and diagonal for roofs and other sloped surfaces. The Quick Job screen is especially inspired, making fast work of crunching measurements for stair, roof, and floor/wall projects. It's a must-have for serious do-it-yourselfers.

A BRAIN FOR BUILDING: The calculator is tuned for common construction measurements. It handles linear, square, and cubic measurements in English and metric units, converting easily between the two. The app lets you store a project's width, height, length, and triangular measurements in memory for easy reference and reuse.

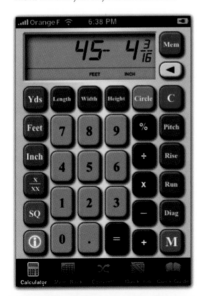

HandyMan Sidekick

$1.99
Version: 1.8
Tech Tree Media

If Carpenter's Helper is a bigger toolkit than you need, check out HandyMan Sidekick, a simple app for managing a handful of common around-the-house project calculations. The app tells you how much paint or wallpaper to buy based on room size, how much flooring you'll need for a project, and the amount of mulch your garden requires. The app also handles simple metric/English unit conversions.

Best App for Picking Paint Colors

ColorSnap

Free
Version: 2.4
Sherwin-Williams

Painting the living room? This handy palette-builder lets you find inspiration in a photo, or match the curtains by snapping a picture. ColorSnap is a product of Sherwin-Williams, and it's aimed at selling you the paint manufacturer's products. But even if you go with another brand, the app is great for quick palette suggestions, and you can always use the provided color recipes to mix your palette with a competitor's blend.

COLOR SAMPLES: Choose a photo from your photo library, or snap one on the spot, and tap the tint you'd like to use as your primary color. Color-Snap shows you the closest matching Sherwin-Williams color, along with two suggestions for secondary colors. Tap the palette to see paint details, including the RGB number that describes its exact color.

SPECTRUM OF OPTIONS: Collect your palettes in one spot by tapping the Save button as you identify colors. The Saved Colors screen lets you review them all in one place. When you've made your pick, tap the Find Store button to find the closest US retailer selling these Sherwin-Williams colors.

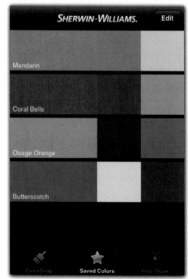

Best App for Real Estate Envy

Zillow

Free
Version: 2.0
Zillow.com

Whether you're looking for a new home or just being a nosy neighbor, Zillow is the best way to find out what a house is worth, what's on the market, and what's recently sold. Zillow has estimates for 88 million homes. You search for all kinds of criteria, but the app's killer feature is using GPS to see prices as you drive through a neighborhood. When you find your dream house(s), save 'em to the app's Favorites screen for future ogling.

COMMUNITY VALUES: Browse home estimates on an aerial map to cruise a neighborhood. The service has estimates for nearly every home in the US, based on public info and recent sales. It's finger-in-the-air stuff but often remarkably accurate. Over 3 million for-sale homes are listed with actual asking prices, along with more casual "make me move" prices that homeowners have posted to Zillow as informal sale offers.

HOUSE PLAN: Find out more about a house on its detail page, including photos, size, and number of rooms. You can include a number of these attributes in the app's search feature, which also lets you save searches. The app alerts you when new homes hit the market matching your search criteria, showing the tally on its iPhone app icon.

Best Apps on the Road

Business or pleasure? Whatever takes you on the road, your iPhone can show you the way. Pack the right apps, and you'll hurtle through airports and far-flung lands, navigating unfamiliar cities and foreign languages like a native. This chapter sends you on a junket of the best travel apps, revealing novel uses for your phone's GPS and on-the-go Internet access to make your trips fly and keep your timetable on the rails.

Your iPhone handily juggles all the **planes, trains, and automobiles** in your itinerary, keeping you organized and on schedule by tracking flights, dodging traffic jams, finding the best subway route, even hailing a taxi. When you arrive at your destination, choose from the best **travel guides** to find the must-see sights or discover obscure treasures not covered in any traditional travelogue. If you don't *parlez-vous* the local lingo, your iPhone or iPod Touch has you covered with translations and phrase books for other **languages.** Armchair travelers can meanwhile transport themselves anywhere instantly, **exploring the world** with a souped-up global map that lets you swoop anywhere.

Pack your bags and download your apps, fellow iPhone traveler; the world is waiting for you.

Photo: Daniel Silveira

Best App for Tracking Flights

FlightTrack Pro

$4.99 for Lite / $9.99 for Pro
Version: 1.2
Mobiata

FlightTrack does exactly what you'd expect, showing the status of any commercial flight around the world. For a $5 premium, the pro version also delivers welcome features for hardcore road warriors: Uncover possible delays by viewing weather and traffic conditions at airports; and if you use the excellent *tripit.com* service to manage your travel (page 200), the pro version automatically monitors those flights for you, too.

VITAL STATS: The Details screen shows your flight's estimated times, as well as terminal and gate information if available. For flights in the air, the app even shows altitude and wind speed, cycling through that info in the top-right corner (where it says "en route" below). Tap Save to stow the flight for future reference. After you do that, the Save button is replaced by a plane icon; tapping it lets you email the flight's status details.

WHERE IN THE WORLD: Tap the Map button to see the flight's progress along its planned route. Some flight trackers do this only for US flights, but FlightTrack maps aircraft around the world. After you've saved a flight to your tracking list by tapping Save, a Refresh icon appears at the bottom of the screen to let you update the map and status details whenever you like.

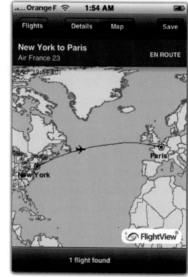

On the Road

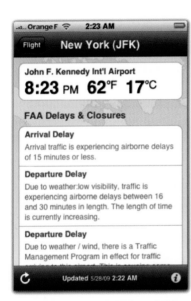

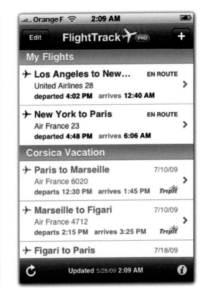

CURRENT CONDITIONS: The pro version lets you view current time, weather, and FAA alerts for arrival and departure airports. (Because the FAA covers only US airports, FlightTrack Pro doesn't provide airport for airports outside the States.)

THE ONES TO WATCH: Saved flights appear in the tracking list on FlightTrack's main screen. Tap a flight to see its status, or click Edit to remove flights from the list. If you use *tripit.com* to manage your travel plans, FlightTrack Pro grabs flights from your account, listing them under their trip names for easy access. Tracking becomes available three days before the flight; later flights are grayed out.

TRAVEL NOTES: Email the current status of any saved flight from its detail or map screen. Flight-Track launches the Mail app with a fresh email message containing all the details—a handy way to alert people on the other end when you'll arrive.

Best App for Organizing Itineraries

TripIt for iPhone

Free
Version: 1.2.1
TripIt

Create tidy, detailed itineraries with TripIt, a hyper-efficient personal travel assistant. The app works with *tripit.com*: After setting up a free account, you forward confirmation emails for all your bookings to TripIt, and the service plucks out the important info, auto-magically converting it into a structured itinerary. The app syncs with your TripIt account, letting you consult the details anywhere, even mid-flight without an Internet connection.

AUTOMATIC ITINERARIES: When you forward confirmation emails to TripIt, the service collects the info into a chronological itinerary, as shown below. The service handles flights, hotels, rental cars, trains, cruises, restaurant reservations, movie and concert tickets, and more. TripIt works with over 250 travel sites and agencies. Basically: If you can book it online, you can add it to your itinerary just by forwarding an email.

TRAVEL DETAILS: Tap an event in the itinerary to see more details. As shown in this hotel reservation, TripIt provides quick-tap links to relevant maps, phone numbers, and websites. (Likewise, TripIt often adds area maps to the main itinerary on days that you arrive in a new city.) You can't edit or delete bookings within the iPhone app; you have to do that from TripIt's website, where you can also add maps, directions, and notes.

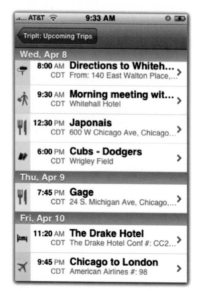

Best App for Tracking Travel Expenses

JetSet Expenses

Free demo / $4.99 full version
Version: 1.4.1
BriteMac

An efficient interface and thoughtfully flexible entry options make JetSet the best way for iPhone-toting road warriors to track expenses. Manage multiple expense reports (for different trips or different clients, for example), and use the app's broad collection of preloaded categories to keep entries organized. The app exports itemized expense reports via email, or you can send them to Google Docs to edit as spreadsheets.

COLORFUL CATEGORIES: Add an expense by tapping a category icon. JetSet starts with the 15 most common categories, but offers over 100 more when you tap the Misc icon. JetSet minimizes typing with one-tap listings of major airlines, hotel chains, and rental car agencies (along with phone numbers). You can similarly insert client or colleague names into the notes field by choosing from your contacts.

THE FULL REPORT: JetSet organizes expense-report entries chronologically; tap one to see the details or make changes. Amounts are color coded as reimbursable (green) or personal (red). You can also mark expenses as billable or not. When you're ready to export the expense report, tap the envelope icon to email it, or tap the broadcast icon to send the report to Google Docs as a spreadsheet.

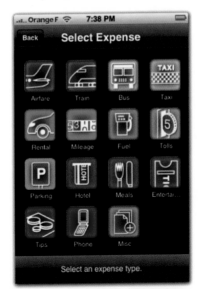

Best Apps for Subway Maps

Subway straphangers can use iPhones to navigate their subterranean commutes. Apps are on offer for most subway systems, with station finders and maps to help ease connections. Many have trip planners, too, accepting start and destination stations to produce travel directions and estimated journey times. If your subway city isn't listed below, take the express to the App Store; most subways are covered.

Tip: You can also use the built-in Maps app to find stations and get subway directions, but the Maps app needs a network and can't help when you're underground.

Berlin

Berlin Trip Planner
Free
Metaquark

Chicago

iTrans Chicago CTA
$1.99
iTrans

London

London Tube Deluxe
$0.99
Malcolm Barclay

Madrid

Madrid Subway
$0.99
Presselite

New York

iTrans NYC Subway
$3.99
iTrans

Paris

RATP Premium
$1.99
faberNovel

San Francisco

iBART Live
$3.99
Pandav

Tokyo

Tokyo Subway Route Map
$0.99
Studio Heat

Washington, DC

iTrans DC Metro
$0.99
iTrans

Best App for Commuter Railways

iTransitBuddy
$4.99
Version: 2.0.1
Blue Technology Solutions

This master of the rails collects the schedules of 20 commuter railroads into a transit bible, a useful reference for daily passengers and occasional visitors alike. Behind the scenes, the app downloads schedule data published online by each rail system, storing the whole schedule on the phone itself, so it's available offline if you need it. Update the schedule when you choose, for the railroads you use.

WHERE TO? Fill out the Trip Planner screen to find the schedule for your selected route. iTransitBuddy offers coverage of 20 commuter lines in New York, Chicago, Boston, Philadelphia, and other cities. This multi-railroad approach is particularly useful in the northeast, where many systems overlap. If you use only one system, single-railroad versions of the app are also available at a discount.

ALL ABOARD: The app shows upcoming trains and helpfully does the time math for you, highlighting the remaining time until departure as you hustle to the station. Tap a train for more details and options, including the ability to add the train route to your favorites for easy reference, or to email the schedule.

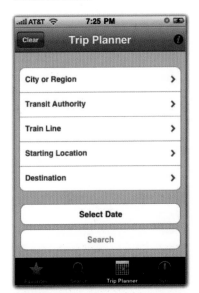

Best App for Hailing a Taxi

NEIGHBORHOOD CABS: Tap the Nearby button to see the closest cab companies. The yellow icon means that the company is part of cab4me's vetted database of cab companies and includes additional info like available car types and payment methods. If cab4me doesn't know about cabs in your area, it hits the web to return a list of phone numbers. Add a company as a favorite, or rate the service to share your experience with others.

cab4me
$1.99
Version: 1.0
Skycoders

Taxi! Cab4me lists recommended cab companies closest to your location; just tap to call. There are lots of all-purpose apps for finding nearby businesses, taxi outfits included, but cab4me has extra info about each company, including service area, which means all listed companies actually serve your location. Customer ratings and payment methods for each company round out the service.

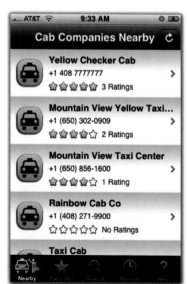

204

+ **HONORABLE MENTION**

Taxi Magic
Free
Version: 1.2
RideCharge

Taxi Magic pulls a taxi out of its hat with the nifty trick of letting you order and pay for a cab, then track its progress to your location, all from your touchscreen. It's amazing, and it really works, providing details about the coming taxi right down to the driver's name. The hitch is that the service is available only in the 25 cities served by RideCharge. If you're not in one of those cab-happy towns, you get a simple list of nearby cab companies and their phone numbers.

Best App for Roadside Discounts

AAA Discounts
Free
Version: 1.0.1
American Automobile Association

The AAA auto club offers more than just an occasional tow. Members can cash in on discounts at 100,000 business in the US and Canada, and this app shows you where to go, mapping the closest participating businesses. It's a convenient way to find restaurants or hotels when you're traveling. Tucked away in the back of the app, you'll also find a screen to get roadside assistance, but the app's main goal is connecting you with bargains.

BARGAINS: The map shows nearby businesses offering AAA discounts (you can see other areas by swiping the map to any location in the US or Canada). Tap a pin to see its name, and tap again for business details, including contact info and the discount offered. Tap List to see a text view of the mapped businesses. The app can also offer driving directions and a highlighted route to the selected location.

FOCUS YOUR SEARCH: You can winnow displayed results by category from the app's Settings screen. Tap an icon to select or deselect the categories; when you return to the map, only matching businesses are displayed.

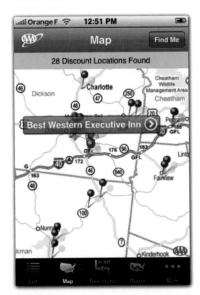

Best Apps for Traditional Guidebooks

Lonely Planet City Guides

$15.99 for each city
Lonely Planet Publications

Lonely Planet is the most prolific and inventive of all travel guidebooks in adapting print material for iPhone. Content for the series' 20 city apps comes straight out of its books, so like the apps' print counterparts, business listings aren't always as fresh as you might find online, but the writerly descriptions of city sights are top-notch—and don't inflict ruinous network fees when roaming abroad.

ON THE MAP: Lonely Planet's apps give their city-guide listings the GPS treatment, with map-based browsing of attractions and businesses; tap one of the map's pins for details about a location. The Nearby screen shows similar information, but in a list view of closest locations. These "what's near me" methods are the only way to browse business listings, making it better for finding something on the go than for planning a day.

BOOK BROWSING: All of the original book's material (apart from business listings) lands in The Book screen, where you drill into the table of contents to find out about the city's history, neighborhoods, culture, and attractions. Searching from this screen scours only the book text, but you can search everything, including business listings, by tapping Search in the dock. You can also purchase additional city guides directly within the app itself.

On the Road

Best App for Custom Guidebooks

HearPlanet
Free / $0.99 full version
Version: 1.7
HearPlanet

HearPlanet is an audio guide that adapts to wherever you go, giving audio commentary on buildings and landmarks around you. Much of the content comes from Wikipedia, and you can choose to read or listen to it. Some items feature human voices, but more obscure locations necessarily rely on text-to-speech robot voices. Still, the effect is like having a knowledgeable companion whispering in your ear as you explore a new place.

POINTS OF INTEREST: HearPlanet's map displays the closest landmarks to your current location or for search results. Tap a pin to reveal its place name and two action arrows; the blue arrow takes you to the topic list for the location, and the white Play icon starts playing audio describing the spot. HearPlanet tracks 250,000 locations around the globe, giving you a practically never-ending audio guide for the whole world.

AUDIO GUIDE: Every location has one or more "topics," mini-chapters of information about the place. Most have an overview topic, shown here, followed by more focused subjects. The Lincoln Memorial, for example, includes topics on "design and construction," "interior," and, tantalizingly, "urban legends." Read the text of each topic, or listen to them to keep your eyes and hands free to better take in your surroundings.

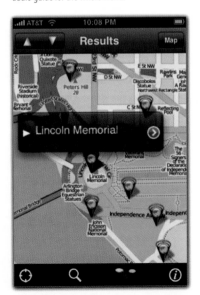

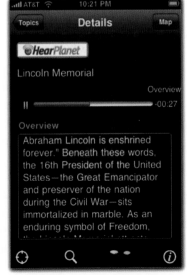

Best Apps for How To Say It

Talking Phrasebooks
$0.99 per language
Coolgorilla

Alas, it turns out that simply speaking English louder doesn't overcome a language barrier. When you travel abroad, it helps to have a few crumbs of the local language. The Talking Phrasebooks series can get you through with seven apps for as many languages. Each offers translations of over 500 common words and phrases for travelers, organized in 40 easy-to-browse categories.

WHAT TO SAY: Search for a keyword to look up a word or phrase in a hurry, and tap it for the translation. You can also browse phrases by category, starting at top-level topics like Food and Drink, Shopping, and Dates and Times and then drilling down into more rarefied topics such as Romance or At the Bar.

HOW TO SAY IT: Select a phrase, and the app shows you its foreign-language translation (non-Western languages get the language's original script, as well as the Western version). Best of all, the app offers audio to coach you how to say the phrase—or simply play it directly for your puzzled waiter. Categories range from "where's the post office" basics to offbeat icebreakers ("I am here to become a sumo wrestler") to more crucial phrases: "I need to contact my embassy."

Best Apps for Looking Up Foreign Words

Ultralingua Dictionaries

$17.99
Ultralingua

At 18 bucks a pop, these translation dictionaries command a premium price, and for good reason. With up to 250,000 entries, these tomes are comprehensive resources for translating words back and forth from other languages, with word definitions, verb conjugations and, helpfully, a numbers translator. Dictionary apps are available for five languages: French, Italian, German, Spanish, and Latin.

LOOK IT UP: Type a foreign word to look up its meaning in English, or vice versa. Here, typing "succeed" in the French translation dictionary yields several French parallels, along with example phrases. Tap a word to find out more about it. For verbs, the dictionary offers conjugations, letting you know how to say a word in the whole gamut of language tenses.

QUICK NUMBERS: The app offers a calculator-like number pad for showing the written equivalent in either English or the other language.

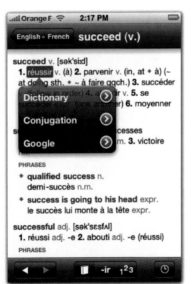

The Best App for Maps

HOME BASE: Tap the location button in the lower-left corner to fly to your current location, marked by the glowing blue orb. Pinch to zoom in or out, drag your finger to pan, and drag with two fingers to rotate. The compass at top right helps you keep your bearings through all this flying, tilting, and spinning. Content icons mark where others have left photos or Wikipedia entries, while food, lodging, and other icons denote businesses. Tap one to find out more.

BEAM ME OVER: The search button lets you teleport anywhere on the planet. Just type in a location, and you fly straight there—a visit to the Matterhorn perhaps. Google Earth captures the height of hills and mountains, so you can zoom down to their base and tilt up to look.

Google Earth
Free
Version: 2.4
Google

Your iPhone's Google-powered Maps app is trusty and reliable, but it's got nothin' on its big brother, Google Earth. Like its desktop counterpart, the iPhone version of Google Earth swoops and soars across the planet's surface in high-resolution 3D, landing at any point you choose. Sprinkled across this landscape are icons representing content like photos, Wikipedia articles, or search results, enabling you to learn, not just look.

Best App for Relief on the Road

Rest Area

$0.99
Version: 1.2
CLO Software

If Google Earth takes you to the soaring heights of the Matterhorn, other mapping apps tend to more... mundane concerns. Rest Area maps the closest rest areas (US only) to your current location or any other place you specify. When you've identified your landing spot, tap it to get details about the available facilities. It's a must-have for any family's road-trip vacation and a handy app for hardgoing drivers who need a break.

ROADSIDE STOP: Map view shows the rest areas in the immediate vicinity, marking your location with a blue cross. Tap a rest area to show its name and location at the top of the screen. Tap the name to get more details about what you'll find there.

USING THE FACILITIES: A rest area's detail screen uses the familiar set of highway icons to show the rest stop's amenities. Tap the "Show on Map" button to flip the rest area into your iPhone's Maps app to get driving directions.

Best Apps for
Your Health

 Flick, swipe, tap! Flick, swipe, tap! And repeat! Your vigorous touchscreen routine provides a workout for more than just your fingers when you turn your iPhone or iPod Touch into a personal trainer and fitness guru. This chapter shows you how to whip you and your iPhone into shape with a lean-and-mean collection of apps for health and fitness.

Start off with a brisk warmup of **general fitness** apps to build a training program, follow a diet, track weight loss, or share your personal fitness feats with others. Then zero in on your favorite exercise with the best apps for specific **sports**—runners and cyclists can track routes and mileage; golfers can find courses and manage scorecards; you can even turn your iPhone or iPod Touch into a virtual treadmill.

Finally, while all this exercise is well and good, there's often nothing better for your physical and mental health than a breath of fresh air. This chapter finishes with an exploration of **the great outdoors,** from trail-finding apps for hikers to bird-watching guides for fans of our fine-feathered friends. So strap on your hiking boots or lace up your cross-trainers, and prepare to break a sweat as you stride through the next few pages.

Photo: Thomas Hawk / thomashawk.com   213

Best App for Dieting and Weight Loss

Lose It!

Free
Version: 1.1
FitNow

The toughest part of a diet isn't so much the portions or menu as it is staying motivated. Lose It! helps you maintain enthusiasm and discipline by turning the dreary details of calorie-counting into a video game: You vs. your calorie budget. Lose It! sets a daily calorie limit based on age, gender, height, and weight-loss goals. Tell it what you eat and how you exercise, and it shows you how well you're meeting your goal.

ON A BUDGET: The My Day screen summarizes each day's calorie intake, showing calories burned and consumed and, the bottom line, whether you stayed under budget. Tap the This Week tab to get a weekly view of your calorie balance, or tap Nutrients to see your consumption of fat, carbohydrates, protein, and the like. Tap Add Food or Add Exercise to log meals or activity for the day.

DIET DETAILS: Record the day's food and exercise from the Log screen, and Lose It! shows the calorie breakdown for each meal and dish, with a running tally of remaining calories in the day's budget. Tap the + button to add food or exercise for the day, or tap Edit to delete items.

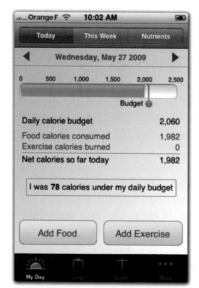

For Your Health

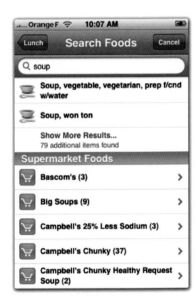

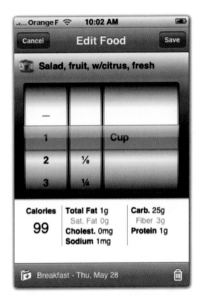

Weightbot

$1.99
Version: 1.3
Tapbots

If recording and counting calories is more work than you care to put into your diet, Weightbot offers a simpler and frankly adorable alternative. The app tracks your daily weight and nothing more, but it does it with whimsical robot sound effects and sleek graphics. Swipe its mechanical band of dates to find the day to enter, tap in your weight, and the app calculates your body mass index for you. Turn your iPhone or iPod Touch sideways, and Weightbot shows a simple chart of your progress toward your desired weight.

STOCKED CUPBOARD: Lose It! provides a big database of food and corresponding calorie counts to speed your data entry. These items include name-brand prepared foods and entrees from popular restaurant chains. You can also add your own custom dishes, detailing the calories and nutrients for each. The log similarly contains a large list of exercise activities to record the day's exercise with just a few taps.

SERVING SIZE: When you add a food, you choose exactly how much you ate, and the entry screen shows the detailed nutritional info for the portion. Lose It! takes note of the foods you eat frequently, stowing them in a My Foods list in the log, so that it's easy to add your standard breakfast, for example.

Best App for Personal Training

iFitness

$1.99
Version: 9.37
Medical Productions

This workout encyclopedia presents over 200 exercises, all with clear photos and plainspoken instructions for how to do each one safely and for best results. Browse by category or muscle group, or assemble exercises into a workout checklist with a suggested routine or your own custom blend. As you sweat your way through your workouts, log and chart your progress in the app's fitness journal, with entry screens tailored for each exercise.

ABS, ARMS, OR ALL OVER: What are you focusing on today? iFitness organizes its exercise categories by body region, plus stretching and cardio for aerobic exercises like running, cycling, step machine, and others. Tap a category to pull up a list of targeted exercises.

A MUSCULAR MENU: Each category includes a big list of exercises. Browse the collection to add variety to a stale workout routine or to target muscle groups you've treated with benign neglect. Scan the list for inspiration, or tap an exercise for photos and complete instructions.

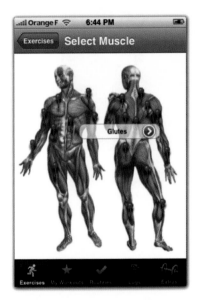

DO IT RIGHT: Be careful with those weights; doing exercises properly will get you the best results and avoid injury. iFitness helps you do just that by illustrating every exercise with one or two clear, uncluttered photos (some have video, too). Double-tap the screen to flip to clearly worded instructions of how (and why) to do each exercise. You can add your own exercises (and your own photos) from the main Exercises screen.

ROUTINES: With more than 200 exercises, iFitness gives you a tasty smorgasbord of options, but possibly more than you can swallow at first. If you're not sure where to start, the Routines screen offers ten workout recipes targeting different goals or profiles. The beginner session, for example, eases you into the basics with fundamental exercises for machines and dumbbells. Assemble your own custom routines in the My Workouts screen.

MUSCLE GROUPS: If you want to tone a specific muscle group, the app lets you zero in on a more focused collection of exercises. Tap the app's diagram of a flayed and pinned man (ouch!) to identify the muscles to work, and then continue to the list of matching exercises.

Best App for Sharing Fitness Feats

Health Cubby

Free demo / $9.99 full version
Version: 1.0.3
App Cubby

Health Cubby sets aside calorie-counting and exercise stats in favor of a big-picture, social approach to fitness. Set weekly diet and exercise goals (run twice, go to the gym three times, allow yourself three "vice" diet splurges). Share your progress with up to seven other Cubby-using buddies for moral support or friendly competition, charting the group's progress toward your weight goals. It's a friendly approach that just might motivate you more than a typical fitness log.

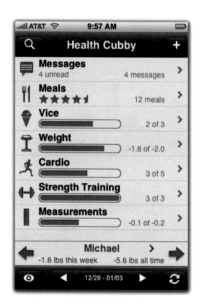

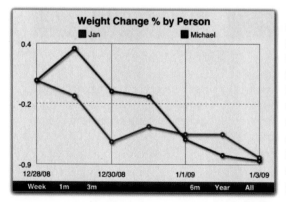

CHART THE CHANGE: Flip Health Cubby on its side to chart the progress of you and your friends toward your weight goal. If you're shy about sharing your weight with the group, Health Cubby instead offers the option to display percentage change. Health Cubby syncs your data online, sharing it with the friends you've approved.

MORE FOREST, LESS TREES: Health Cubby encourages you to focus on big-picture goals rather than nitty-gritty details of weight reps, mileage, or calories. Add brief entries when you eat or exercise, giving meals a star rating (1 for junk food, 5 for ultra-healthy) instead of calorie counts. The app shows how you're doing against your weekly goals, or you can check stats for a friend or the whole group.

Best App for Reducing Stress

Breath Pacer

$2.99
Version: 1.03
Larva Labs

Just breathe. That's what Breath Pacer helps you do, prompting you to breathe at slow, measured intervals to reduce stress and, it claims, ease depression or insomnia. Okay: Three bucks to practice how to breathe? Chances are you can figure out *that* without your iPhone. But if having the app actually makes you pause to take a breath—or several very long breaths—then hey, that's money well spent.

BREATHE IN, BREATHE OUT: The app suggests breath intervals based on your height (a good indicator, apparently, of your body's cardiovascular demands), but you can change those any time in the app's settings. Choose how long you want to inhale and exhale.

RAINFALL: Breath pacer gives you simple audio and visual cues for pacing your breathing. The bar rises as you inhale and drops as you let it out. The sound of rain rises and falls in sync with the bar, which means you don't have to look at the screen, so you can tune out for a few minutes and breathe deeply to the sound of rainfall.

Best App for Running

RunKeeper

Free lite version / $9.99 full version
Version: 1.6.0.10
FitnessKeeper

This nifty GPS-powered running log tracks your location, providing pace, distance, and altitude info, even mapping your running route. RunKeeper syncs to the app's website, where you can analyze, chart, and share stats to your healthy heart's content. Because it relies on GPS, the app works only outside (sorry treadmillers), and iPhone limitations keep it from tracking your run in the background (you're on pause if the phone rings).

NICE PACE: The app shows your speed, time, and distance as you run, charting your pace in minute intervals. Tap the icon at top left to lock the screen and keep yourself from tapping the Stop or Pause button accidentally; the screen switches to landscape view with big, easy-to-read numbers. In the pro version, tapping the screen prompts RunKeeper to speak your current stats, dodging any clumsy fumbling to check your time.

RUNNING ROUTE: View maps of your current and past runs, handy for navigating an unfamiliar city or race course. RunKeeper lets you load photos and Twitter-like notes along your running route, marked with gray pins on the map. The app hangs onto this info for all your runs, but the real nitty-gritty historical review happens at the app's website, *runkeeper.com*, where you can chart, map, and share your running routes and photos.

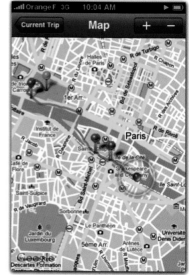

For Your Health

C25K

$2.99
Version: 1.3
Alex Stankovic

C25K is shorthand for "Couch to 5K," a popular online running program for new runners (which, coincidentally, was created by your humble author, though he had no hand in this app). The program shepherds non-runners through easy walking/jogging workouts, gradually building to a 5K distance. It's an effective way to ease into running without the unhappy discomfort that so many people associate with it. The routine requires a mix of timed walking and jogging, and this app handles the details for you, giving you audio prompts for when to walk or run while you listen to your own music in the background.

DAY BY DAY: The C25K running program unfolds over nine weeks, with three outings per week. Tap the workout that you want to run, and afterward the app marks it complete. You can do a day over by tapping the Edit button to remove the checkmark.

WALK, RUN: Each day includes a brief description of the workout with big, easy-to-read numbers of your time overall and for the current walk/run segment. Audio alerts tell you when to run or walk, and also when you hit the halfway mark so you know when to turn around.

Best App for a Virtual Treadmill

iTreadmill

Free demo / $1.99 full version
Version: 2.0.0
Ricky Amano

iTreadmill is a good alternative or complement to RunKeeper to help runners and walkers measure pace and distance. The app uses the motion detector of your iPhone or iPod Touch to turn the device into a pedometer that counts the number of steps you take. After a bit of up-front calibration, the app is remarkably accurate and, unlike RunKeeper, you can use it indoors, even running in place to create a virtual treadmill.

GET MOVING: Start, stop, and pause buttons trigger iTreadmill to start your run, tracking your pace and distance (or virtual distance if you're running in place). If you've given the app your weight, it also estimates the number of calories you've burned. Before using the app, it's a good idea to calibrate it to your stride length by tapping the "cal" button at the top right.

PERFECT PACE: Work your thumb across the dial at the top right to set the pace of your run or walk. When you turn on the pacer, the app makes a ticking rhythm to pace your footfalls. If you keep your normal stride length and match the app's rhythm, you'll hit the speed you're after.

For Your Health

222

Best App for Golfing

GolfCard
$7.99
Version: 1.11.1
Senygma

Hit the links with this all-in-one app for golfers of every level. GolfCard includes a score card, a GPS range finder, and a bevy of personal stats including calculated handicap. The app has online access to info for over 20,000 courses, many of them with maps to let you use the app's range finder. If your course isn't included, the easy course builder lets you add it before tee off.

GOAL IN SIGHT: Set up a round by downloading the info for your course into GolfCard and adding the player details. GolfCard remembers courses and players, so setup is a one-time deal. The app's score card lets you keep things simple or add lots of details (chips, sandshots, putts, penalties, and more).

Golf by Zagat
$4.99
Version: 1.0.0
Handmark

Traveling golfers will appreciate this app's reviews of 1200 US golf courses, including public, semi-private, and resort courses. In traditional Zagat style, the app gives number scores for course, facilities, service, and value, but the meat comes from the snippets of quotes from actual golfers who know the course. ("Heaven can't be more beautiful," says one golfer of the course at Pebble Beach.) It's not a comprehensive guide, but it's a handy way to discover a region's top greens.

Best App for Cycling

Cychosis

$4.99
Version: 1.7.0
Ron Forrester

Cychosis is a clean and efficient training log for bikers and cyclists, letting you record nitty-gritty details about daily rides as well as big-picture goals for the year. Once you've churned out the miles, you can roll back through your data in graphs charting the distances, average speed, and total times of your rides. If that's not enough number-crunching for you, you can export your data to a spreadsheet file to massage it on your own.

YOUR RIDES: The Rides screen summarizes your workouts for the week, month, year, or all time. Flip Cychosis to landscape view to see your charts, or tap the + button to add a new ride. You can keep entries simple with just the basic time and distance, or pour it on with heart rate, cadence, course gradient, and more. The app plugs into your Twitter account, too, so you can optionally tweet your rides as you add them to the journal.

RESOLUTIONS: Cychosis lets you add any number of distance goals and track your progress toward them from the Goals screen. You can likewise track the number of miles and rides you've put on your bike(s), and stow info on common routes for fast entry of distance, elevation, and more.

For Your Health

Bike Your Drive

Free
Version: 1.0
Global Motion Media

Track how many calories you've burned (and the carbon emissions you *haven't*) with this app that tracks and maps your ride via GPS, a low-key parallel to RunKeeper for cyclists (page 220). The app is part of a campaign by outdoor outfitter REI to encourage commuters to bike instead of drive, and it has some social features built in to help bikers spread the word to friends and family. The app maps and posts your cycling route at *everytrail.com,* an online community for sharing travel stories, including photos you take along your ride.

CYCLING COMMUTER: As you ride, Bike Your Drive shows your speed and distance, along with estimates of the carbon offset and gas money you've saved by riding your bike instead of driving. It takes into account your body's fuel, too, with a tally of calories burned. Tap the Photo button to add a photo to your ride. When you post your ride to *everytrail.com,* the photo will appear at that location of your bike route.

SAVED TRIPS: Bike Your Drive saves your trips future browsing; flip through maps and photos as you go. You can share your trip maps via Twitter, Facebook, or email.

Best App for Hiking

Trails

Free demo / $3.99 full version
Version: 2.0
Felix Lamouroux

Trails is a GPS tracker that's perfectly tuned for capturing and sharing your adventures. While other apps (like GPS Kit or MotionX GPS) are thicker with technical features, Trails is ideal for casual mapping fans who still take their trails seriously. The app records your "tracks," and you can also use it to follow the downloaded tracks of others. One hitch: Trails has to run constantly to track your route, a big battery drain for long hikes.

TRACKER: As Trails follows you, it shows the time, pace, and distance of your outing, similar to other GPS apps covered in this chapter. Snap a picture to tag it to your route, and drop waypoints along the way to label points of interest. Once complete, you can post and share your map online at *everytrail.com*, or download and follow the maps of others from a variety of mapping sites.

LOCAL MAPS: Review your tracks on either road maps or topographic maps like the one shown here. Unlike Google Maps, which require a constant Internet connection to view the map, Trails downloads the map for your trip ahead of time and saves it on your iPhone, so you don't need an Internet connection while you're on the trail.

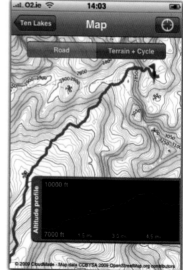

Best App for Bird Watching

iBird Explorer Plus

$19.99
Version: 1.6.1
Mitch Waite Group

While you're out on that hike, get cozy with your area's winged population. iBird Explorer Plus is an interactive field guide to nearly 1000 North American birds, including gorgeous hand-drawn illustrations, 1800 photos, and audio birdcalls loud enough to attract the real thing. All this lush media makes for a big app, so make some room on your iPhone or iPod.

FEATHERED FRIENDS: *iBird Explorer Plus* helps you identify birds by searching by name, location, shape, size, and habitat; results are displayed with icons to help you get a visual fix on your subject. Tapping the bird brings up its detail page, including an Audubon-like illustration. If you want something less expansive, other editions of iBird Explorer are available, focusing on smaller North American regions or "backyard" birds.

STOMPING GROUNDS: Every bird's detail page includes a map showing its range. There's much more, too: Listen to the bird's birdcall, view photos, read facts, and info so detailed that you'll discover what the bird eats and the color of its eggs.

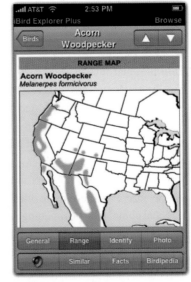

Best App for Weather Forecasts

AccuWeather.com

Free
Version: 2.0
AccuWeather

Your iPhone's built-in Weather app is fine for quick-and-dirty forecasts, but when you crave more detail, Accu-Weather provides the best weather info for iPhone. With animated radar and satellite images, hour-by-hour forecasts for the next 15 hours, and 15-day forecasts, the app provides lots of detail about what's happening now and well into the future. Check out local news and videos, or cast your eye abroad for international weather.

WHAT'S IT LIKE OUT THERE? The app's home screen gives you a quick update of current conditions with a photo to match. Tap the tabs at the bottom of the screen to see a forecast for your selected area (or tap the crosshair at top left to switch to your current location).

RADAR AND SATELLITE: See the weather in motion with *AccuWeather.com's* radar and satellite animations. Severe weather in your area flips an indicator in the dock to show you alerts and warnings. More modest indicators show up in the Risk screen, where you can review chances of severe weather, and lifestyle indices like pollen levels.

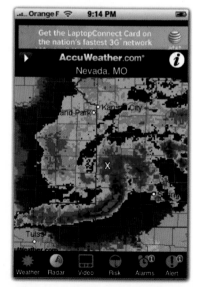

App Index

Try the online edition free for 45 days

Get the information you need when you need it, with Safari Books Online. Safari Books Online contains the complete version of the print book in your hands plus thousands of titles from the best technical publishers, with sample code ready to cut and paste into your applications.

Safari is designed for people in a hurry to get the answers they need so they can get the job done. You can find what you need in the morning, and put it to work in the afternoon. As simple as cut, paste, and program.

**To try out Safari and the online edition of the above title FREE for 45 days,
go to www.oreilly.com/go/safarienabled and enter the coupon code MLOEGDB.**

To see the complete Safari Library visit:
safari.oreilly.com